WRECK FISHING

Clive Gammon

Colour plates by Keith Linsell

OSPREY PUBLISHING LIMITED

First published in 1975 by
Osprey Publishing Ltd., 137 Southampton Street,
Reading, Berkshire
Member Company of the George Philip Group

Series Design: Norman Ball and Paul Bowden

Filmset and printed Offset Litho in Great Britain by
Cox & Wyman Ltd., London, Fakenham and Reading

ISBN 0 85045 219 8

I. WRECK FISHING

The tanker foundered 25 miles south-east of Plymouth on a cold, autumn day in 1941, a single torpedo shearing away most of its bow. She slipped under the Atlantic swell and settled on a bottom of muddy sand 120 feet below the surface. As soon as she touched the sea bed a strange transformation began. Her metal sides began to corrode. But at the same time spores of seaweed floating in the water took hold on her, grotesquely-shaped sea anemones found a hold on the hull. The spring tides swept her under and gouged out a trench beyond her stern. A new pattern of currents formed, eddying around the wreck just as the flow of a stream changes as it encounters a boulder. As the years passed weeds and barnacles began to grow in great profusion, softening its profile. But they were not the only forms of marine life that sought her out. Making their way through ventilators and torn-off hatch covers, an army of conger eels had populated the below-decks zone, some of them small fish of twenty or thirty pounds but a few weighing five or six times as much, great, black, blunt-headed creatures which swam out over the long, flat decks when the tide eased, to search for prey. A little above them were serried ranks of ling, somewhat eel-like in proportions but thicker in the body and mottled like cod. There were big-eyed pouting and a heavy cod or two, but most striking of all, holding station against the tide and stacked up to mid-water, was a vast shoal of pollack, hundreds strong. Amongst them and above them were red sea-bream — scarlet, gold, and silver in reality — that were almost as numerous. On the sand around the wreck, attracted by the scour of tide that made it a natural harbour for food, were other species — turbot, plaice, sole, huge angler-fish that looked like green and brown mottled rocks. And there were rarities too: dusky perch and stone basse with spiked dorsal fins erect. And,

because this was high summer, everywhere from a fathom below the surface to the sea bed itself there were mackerel, thousands, and thousands of them.

For thirty years and more, the wreck lay there without anyone being aware of its presence, not even the navy hydrographer whose job it is to mark wrecks on the Admiralty charts. He could hardly be blamed for that. In the Western Approaches, after the U-boat wolf packs had finished, there were hundreds of wrecks that probably will never be charted.

In the end, though, this one was. A fifty-foot trawler making a last sweep before heading back into Brixham fouled its nets in the barnacled superstructure, at a loss of hundreds of pounds to the skipper. But he would be unlikely ever to lose gear again on the same wreck because as soon as his nets had gone fast he had checked out the co-ordinates on the Decca Navigator with which his vessel was equipped. And he was able to recoup a small percentage of his losses when he made harbour again by passing on the co-ordinates to the skipper of a sea angling boat that headed out from the Barbican in Plymouth whenever the weather was right and there was a full load of fishermen booked. It meant a long haul for him though and he had to wait until he could muster enough anglers willing to pay for a forty-eight-hour trip. But that part was not really difficult: experienced men would know the kind of harvest that waited for them.

And so in the last light of evening the angler-laden boat headed out for the distant mark. It would anchor up near the Eddystone for a while and fish congers, then it would make a run for the new wreck with the intention of hitting it at first light, when the tide would be running fast on the flood.

Even five years ago such an ambition would have been laughable. Even with an echo-

sounder and an indication on the chart as to where the wreck lay, it might be hours before it was located. Wreck fishing, unless it was over a wreck that was within sight of shore landmarks and could therefore be located easily, was impossible until the Decca Navigational system revolutionized the whole sport, enabling skippers to pinpoint a couple of square yards of sea far out of sight of land.

As the wreck-fishing boat turned into the swell heading for the torpedoed tanker, the anglers crowded into the wheel-house to watch the green, purple, and red lights of the Navigator winking in the darkness. 'Twenty more minutes', said the skipper. And, because of the precision of his electronic guide, he was being perfectly precise himself. In twenty minutes the big Kelvin Hughes echo-sounder was switched on and the total reliability of the Navigator was demonstrated. Instead of the gently undulating sea bed that would have shown up anywhere else, the written record of the sounder showed a dramatic

a danbuoy over, a big, orange sphere that would mark the bow of the wreck and would save him locating it again. And he looked carefully around from horizon to horizon. Decca Navigators are expensive to hire: they cost £500 a year. And it is by no means unknown for Decca-less craft to sneak out to sea behind a properly-equipped skipper and poach the wreck that he has located.

But now it was time to start fishing. The anglers, once they knew they were going to drift, had started rigging their gear. Most of them used plastic lures that imitated sand-eels, three at a time. Others tied on heavy chromed 'pirks', lures that originated in Scandinavia and which were designed for attracting and hauling big cod commercially. The skipper was concentrating on the flickering stylus of the echo-sounder. Then he yelled over the throb of the diesel, 'We're right over her now! Get amongst them! And watch your gear in the wreck.' Eight sets of lures slid down fast and within seconds eight rods keeled over hard as fish hit without caution. It was all action for the anglers but the skipper had to work even harder. He had hauled up the hatches of the fish-hold and as the first angler, his catch looming in the clear water, shouted for the gaff, he was at his side swinging aboard big, olive-skinned pollack, twelve- and fourteen-pounders, three at a time. Within ten minutes more than a hundredweight of pollack had come aboard. Already anglers had lost lures and big fish in the wreck itself but the ones that had not been put out of action had time for another drop before the effective drift was over and the boat had lost contact with the shoals. The skipper slammed the craft into gear again, brought her round, and squared her up for another drift. 'Down you go again!' he shouted and, panting a little now, for hauling two or three big pollack through twenty fathoms is not easy work, the anglers let down their gear again. If it had been any other form of hard labour they would have demanded to have been paid for it, instead of themselves paying for the privilege.

There were more passes at the pollack. Amongst them were one or two coalfish, nothing

steepling, a series of peaks and valleys that represented the profile of the wreck as the boat motored over her.

The skipper checked the run of tide and wind: if the wreck was to be fished properly then full account had to be taken of them. The tide was still running hard and what wind there was ran with it. There was no question of anchoring yet. 'We'll drift!' he shouted, going up-tide and swinging the boat beam on to where the wreck lay. Before any fishing started, though, he slipped

5

like as many as would be over the wreck in January but enough of them to make it clear that they pulled harder even than the pollack, crash-diving again and again even against the strain of 50 lb. test nylon. There would be red bream too, fighting like fish twice their weight but still not enough to make much impact on the wreck-fishers' tackle even if they could grab the big hooks. One angler, looking perhaps for a little variation, added a strip of mackerel to the treble hook of his pirk and let it down very quickly to try to get through the shoals of ravenous pollack. He succeeded: his bait was taken with a heavy, thumping resistance by a fish that did not crash-dive but fought sullenly all the way up — a ling of maybe 30 lb. Seasoned as they were the eight anglers had experienced nothing like this: they were fishing a virgin wreck for the first time, a vast fish fortress that had never been attacked before. But they were secretly glad, perhaps, when the skipper signalled that it was time for a change. The tide had begun to ease now and it was going to be possible to anchor. That meant different tackle and different tactics and a welcome respite from trying to stand upright on a heaving deck and at the same time fight heavy fish far below. Once more the skipper had to bring all his craft and experience into play judging the exact moment to let down the anchor so that his boat would settle just up-tide of the wreck making it possible for the anglers' baits running down the tide to make contact with the tanker.

Not only the tackle but the fish would change now. The lures had been taken off. In their place short running traces with a wire link at the end and armed with massive 12/0 hooks had been rigged. For a short while, though, the anglers helped the skipper to feather for mackerel on light rods. The bait boxes had to be full for once the action started there would be no time to feather again.

Every angler had his own preference about the way he cut bait. Some preferred just a mackerel head, others a whole fish, and others a thick fillet from the side. When they were mounted the baits were let down slowly — a fast drop and the trace might become tangled before it hit bottom. It was a pleasant change to sit and fish and wait for a bite, though the respite did not last long. First one then a second rod bent over. The congers were on the move. When they

surfaced, though, they were not, comparatively speaking, as fine fish as the pollack had proved to be. Instead they ran between 20 and 30 lb., fine prizes for the inshore angler but small fry where wreck fishermen are concerned. Para-doxically, a virgin wreck rarely yields big conger. The 100 lb. plus fish are there, of course, but they are inevitably beaten to the bait by the smaller more active fish. It is a 'fished out' wreck that produces the biggest congers — but more of this later on. Conger were not the only fish to come aboard. There were almost as many ling which, if anything, fight harder, but curiously are not so prized by many wreck fishermen. And one angler, who was not all that happy to use heavy gear and catch big eels, had stationed himself right in the stern of the boat and was drifting a thin strip of mackerel weighted by just a couple of ounces of lead, well down-tide. He was catching bream and pollack no bigger than the fish that everyone was landing when the boat was drifting, but on the light gear he was using he was getting far better sport than when he was dropping straight down into the shoals with a heavy lead and multiple lures.

Finally, when the tide became completely slack, the action with the congers ceased. And the skipper hauled anchor, shaping-up for a short drift over the sands that surround the wreck with the anglers using their bottom fishing gear. They struck lucky right away. There was a turbot which must have weighed more than 20 lb. and a couple of good cod. And the angler in the bow was into something that had him heaving and panting for nearly fifteen minutes before he could bring it to the surface — a huge, ugly lump of a 50 lb. angler-fish, its enormous head vastly disproportionate to its body.

That night, when the boat tied up again to the Barbican pontoon and the weary anglers clam-bered ashore and the catch was weighed, there was more than a ton and a half of fish, a catch that a few years ago would have been beyond any angler's wildest dream. Wreck fishing, 1970s style, is something quite new in sea angling. It has been criticized as being too excessive a fish kill, but even with its obvious scope results have been exaggerated — you do not break a British record every time you go out, even on a virgin wreck. One thing is certain though: it is a totally fascinating form of angling which has no parallel in any other branch of the sport.

2. MODERN AIDS TO WRECK FISHING

A day's wreck fishing is certainly considerably more expensive for the angler than a day at any other form of salt-water sport. Whereas a trip aboard an ordinary angling charter boat might cost around £3 a head, in the case of a wreck trip the charge will be at least £5, and private charter about £40 a day, almost twice as much as hiring a normal off-shore fishing craft. The reason for this lies in the more expensive and more sophisticated equipment a wreck-fishing boat has to have aboard it, the most important single item of which is the Decca Navigator.

It might seem odd in a fishing book to write about complex radio equipment and I have no intention of going into the kind of detail that would only interest an electronics engineer. But, because it adds enormously to the interest of a wrecking trip to know what is going on in the wheel-house where green, purple, and red lights are winking mysteriously on a bulkhead console, I am going to outline now just how the skipper uses this particular aid to put his anglers precisely on a wreck lying far off-shore. Incidentally, the skipper himself need not be an electronics wizard: the system is so simple to read that you can learn how to use it in less than an hour.

In the photograph you will see that prominent in the layout are three dials (two of which are actually used at one time in getting a fix) called 'Decometers'. These work in conjunction with land-based transistors and a special navigation chart. Not all the seas of the world are covered by the Decca system but all of the coastal waters of Western Europe are, and there is no doubt that eventually all the important, i.e. much travelled, coastal waters of the world will be added to the system. Thus, if it is simply a question of discovering your precise position, you simply read off the co-ordinates displayed on the Decometers and relate them to the navigation chart. It makes no difference if it is night or day, whether the sea is flat calm or there is a gale blowing; neither does the roll, pitch, nor list of the vessel reflect the reading. More commonly, however, the skipper will want to use his Navigator to lead him to an exact fix on the chart and clearly this is done by starting out with the co-ordinates and working back. In other words he has to so steer the boat that the Decometer readings eventually match up with the co-ordinates for the wreck's position which he starts out with. The accuracy is quite extraordinary. The boat can be positioned within one hundredth of a 'Decca line', or just a couple of metres of the wreck. If you are technically

The Decca Navigator Mark 21 receiver.

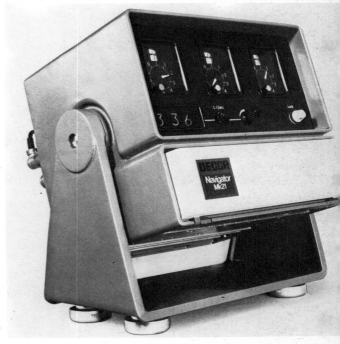

Decca track plotter.

inclined you may be interested in this description of the system for which I am indebted to Decca Navigator Company Limited.

The Decca Navigator is a hyperbolic radio navigation system operated in conjunction with ground transmitter chains working in the 70—130 kHz frequency band. The signals can be received at distances of several hundred miles from the transmitters. The characteristic high accuracy of the Decca Navigator System results from its hyperbolic geometry and its use of the phase comparison principle.

A Decca Chain consists of three pairs of transmitters, a common central master and three outlying slave stations 50—100 miles from the master, designated Red, Green, and Purple. Neither the symmetry of the chain nor the master to slave distance is critical. Transmitted signals are in the form of continuous unmodulated radio waves, slave signals being phase-locked to the master. The frequencies of the unmodulated continuous radio

waves transmitted from the master and slaves are harmonically related to a fundamental value 'f', which is not transmitted but which is roughly 14 kHz, the exact value varying from chain to chain. Phase synchronization of master and slave transmissions creates a pattern of hyperbolic position lines along which the phase difference between master and slave is constant.

Position fixing, carried out by the Decca marine receiver, consists basically of identifying position lines by phase comparison carried out at a common multiple (or sub-multiple) frequency.

If all that is not crystal clear to you don't worry, the important thing is that the system works. Incidentally, there is a further development in the Decca system which has not yet come through to sea angling boats but will no doubt one day be part of their equipment. That is an actual graphic record of the voyage — in other words a track plotter which gives a continuous record of the ship's position (see above). This piece of equipment makes it even more easy to record trips which can be analysed after-

Conger (*Conger conger*)

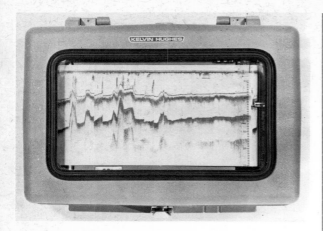

WHAT IS 'WHITE LINE' RECORDING?

The purpose of 'white line' presentation is to pick out echo traces from fish shoals on or very near the seabed. It is often difficult using normal recording, to distinguish fish traces from the bottom echoes.

With the recorder switched to 'white line', the bottom echo appears as a thin dark line on the record chart with a blank portion, or 'white line', immediately following it. Echoes from fish on or near the seabed cause the line to thicken. If fish are present in significant quantities, the echo traces will show as shady patches above the line.

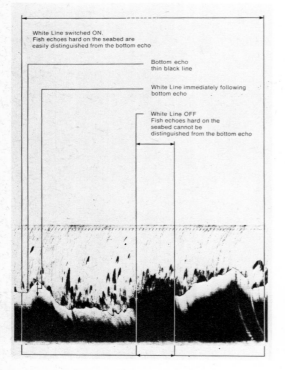

White Line switched ON.
Fish echoes hard on the seabed are easily distinguished from the bottom echo

Bottom echo
thin black line

White Line immediately following
bottom echo

White Line OFF
Fish echoes hard on the seabed cannot be distinguished from the bottom echo

wards. In other words you can file your fishing marks!

The Navigator is not the only piece of electronic equipment that a wrecking boat has to have. Because a wreck may be very large as, for example, the famous aircraft carrier wrecked off South Devon, a sophisticated echo-sounder is also necessary to show up the positions of fish shoals on it, and also the direction in which it is lying. Once the Navigator has taken the skipper to the wreck the sounder comes into play and, when the boat is drifting at least, it is kept switched on continuously so that the skipper can manoeuvre the boat to optimum advantage.

Such echo-sounders are not the simple devices with which many in-shore boats are equipped, the least sophisticated of which simply gives a 'blip' indicating depth. Even the rather more expensive devices which give a profile of the bottom by means of a stylus running over a moving roll of paper are not adequate. The wreck skipper who wants to make a firstclass reputation for himself needs a high-sensitivity fish finder, a good example of which is the Kelvin Hughes MS 37 or MS 39 (see above left).

The main advantage that such models as these have over the inexpensive graphic-record sounders is that they incorporate the 'white line' system which makes it possible to distinguish between the echoes made by the bottom of the sea and by fish that are swimming on or close to the sea bed (see below left). Such instruments are not cheap and can cost from £400 upwards — indeed a really sophisticated model such as is used on commercial fishing boats can be as expensive as £2 500.

A wrecker will also carry ship-to-shore radio and one or two boats are also equipped with radar for safer navigation. Additionally there will be all the safety equipment specified by Board of Trade and local harbour regulations — a life raft amongst them. Thus a properly equipped wreck-fishing boat represents a lot of money and it is not surprising that charges are comparatively high, although the quality of sport, at least expressed in terms of numbers caught, is far greater than what is to be obtained in normal sea angling craft.

'White line' recording.

3. THE FISH OF THE WRECKS

1. The sea breams

Because there are bigger, more prestigious species around wrecks the sea breams don't get very much publicity as sport fish. But sporting fish they are, and it is only the angler's traditional obsession with size that prevents them from getting the reputation they deserve. As I hope to show later, so long as tackle is suitably scaled down, the wreck fisherman can expect just as much in the way of an exciting fight from a 4 lb. bream as he can from a 15 lb. pollack. There are certain problems, of course, when you are fishing light tackle into a concentration of thousands of fish: for instance you will certainly lose gear when you encounter heavier species on tackle that was only intended for bream. But such losses must be counted part of the game.

On West Country wrecks it is the red sea bream *(Pagellus bogaraveo)* which is by far the commonest representative of the Sparidae, though farther east in the English Channel black bream *(Spondyliosoma cantharus)* become proportionately more significant. Both, however, react in very similar ways to sea angling methods and once we come to consider bream fishing over wrecks I don't propose to distinguish between the two. Meanwhile, before coming to angling techniques, let's hear a little about the fish themselves.

It is worth saying first of all that both species have made a remarkable comeback in post-war years. During the 1930s sea bream almost disappeared from the coastal waters of Britain and Ireland and in fact before the war the author of the sea fishing volume in the well-known sporting Lonsdale library wrote apologetically that he was including a chapter on sea bream even though he 'remained unconvinced, and never expected to see the time when black bream fishing would be anything like it was in its palmy days'. However he decided to do his best 'in the hope that the fishing may improve in the future and an account of the methods found successful in the past may be of use'. Happily the writer was too pessimistic. Black bream returned to the eastern English Channel in the early 1950s and although they were at first concentrated on certain reefs of the Sussex coast, they rapidly spread until now they are

A fine black bream surfaces . . .

. . . and is safely brought aboard.

being caught as far east as Kent and as far west as Cornwall and Cardigan Bay.

Much the same story is true of the red sea bream. In many places in the West Country and in Ireland there were sea angling marks with names like 'Bream Rocks' or 'Bream Head' which were puzzling to the anglers in the immediate post-war days because never a bream was to be found on them. But late in the 1950s — rather later than in the case of black bream — the species began to return in greater and greater numbers. No one has ever quite accounted for their mysterious disappearance. Some blamed excessive trawling (although it is only the red species that is the subject of any sizeable commercial fishery) but, although commercial exploitation may have had something to do with the diminution of numbers, the main factor may well have been the disappearance of a certain seaweed, *Zooastra*, which the bream favours. Whatever the truth, the good news is that bream are now plentiful in our waters.

The red sea bream is one of the most beautiful fish in the sea. In profile it is homely enough, high shouldered, somewhat flattened vertically, and having the spined dorsal fin characteristic of the genus. It is its colouration that really makes it a delight to see as it comes inboard. The overall colour is a glorious orange-red which lightens towards the belly to silver and pink; on the shoulder of the fish there is also a dark patch, a 'St. Peter's thumb' mark similar to that on the haddock. Some trawlermen, indeed, call the species Jerusalem haddock. They are summer fish, coming within the scope of the angler from, roughly, June until the end of September or the beginning of October. In normal circumstances they are very much fish of reefs and rocky bottoms but they have adapted very well indeed to wrecks and, as in the case of most other species, the average size of wreck specimens considerably exceeds that of fish taken in more natural habitats.

We don't know a great deal about the spawning habits of bream. Very small red bream sometimes become abundant in shallow water especially late in the summer and these 2—3-inch long fish are generally reckoned to be the fry of that year. No one has managed to identify the eggs of the sea bream in British waters, so where and when spawning takes place is still a matter for controversy, though many anglers are pretty

convinced that their summer inshore migration is for this purpose. However, Alwyne Wheeler considers that spawning occurs in deep water, over 55 fathoms, in late summer and autumn around the British Isles. In other words they migrate *from* inshore waters for the purpose of spawning. The growth rate is fairly slow. A good sized (from the angling point of view) bream of, say, 18 inches long may be as much as fourteen years old.

As any angler will tell you, once bream are in a feeding mood they will take most baits, a reflection on their pretty well omnivorous diets. They will take small fish, starfish, crabs, and even seaweed, and are clearly highly adaptable. The famous ichthyologist, Thaddeus Dunn of Mevagissey, noted how when a ship laden with wheat was wrecked off Cornwall, bream that were later caught in the neighbourhood were found to be crammed full of the grain.

The black sea bream looks like a slightly more streamlined (scientists would say 'compressed') version of the red species, but it differs strongly in colouration. Really, 'black' is quite the wrong adjective although after death the fish lose their brilliant colouration and assume a dark grey hue. Above, black bream are a rich purple-blue. The sides are silvery-blue, and six or seven dark vertical bars extend down from the back. Sometimes the tail and pectoral fins have a yellow tinge. This description hardly conveys the flashing brilliance of the live fish, made up of blue, silver, and purple lights. Like the red bream, the black bream is one of the most beautiful fish in the sea.

It is a rather more localized species than the red bream, and its numbers thin out very much the farther west you go: there have only been a handful of authenticated instances from Irish waters, for example, and none farther north than the Menai Straits.

We know even less of the biology of the black sea bream than we do of the red, although it turns up in British waters rather earlier than the latter does, sometimes in the month of April. The shoals then are very concentrated and begin to break up towards the end of June. This is when spawning probably takes place and it is only then that numerically large catches can be made. From the wreck fisherman's point of view, however, the species becomes of interest later in the summer and he is then concerned not with shoaling black bream but with odd large specimens. The male black bream actually makes a nest — or at least a depression in the sea bed — and guards the fertilized eggs very much in the manner of a stickleback.

The black bream seems to be a slightly less catholic feeder than the red species, though this need scarcely worry the angler for most offerings are happily taken — these are usually small lugworm or fish strips. The theory was once held that black bream did nothing but browse on seaweeds and algae but there seems no doubt that more characteristically it takes shrimp, small crabs, and fish.

Other species of bream occasionally turn up in British waters and some of them resemble our two most common species quite strongly. Amongst them are the pandora *(Pagellus erythrinus)*, the gilt-head *(Aparus aurata)*, and the dentex *(Dentex dentex)*. The details which will help you to make an identification are too complex to be included here — they involve fin ray counts and measurements of eye diameters and a close look at the pattern of teeth. If you catch a bream which seems to you unusual, it is best to check the species in either Wheeler's *The Fishes of the British Isles and North West Europe* or Kennedy's *The Sea Angler's Fishes*.

The red bream is a somewhat larger species than the black bream. The British record for the red is 7 lb. 8 oz., taken in 1925 by A. F. Bell of Fowey — a fish of the pre-wreck era, notice — and the record black is a 6 lb. 1 oz. fish taken in Devon waters in 1969 by F. W. Richards. The biggest red bream taken in the waters of the British Isles, however, is the present Irish record, an enormous specimen of 9 lb. 6 oz. caught by Paddy Maguire off Valentia Island. When it was first reported in 1963 it was assumed to have been a dentex, but examination by a zoologist showed it to be a true red sea bream. The average angler, however, would be well pleased with a 5 lb. red or a 3½ lb. black bream — useful weights for roughly describing a 'specimen' of either.

Bream fishing over a wreck is best carried out when the other anglers are intent on catching heavy ling or conger. It is very important, though, to make sure that you keep well out of their way since you will be using very light tackle which will drift at a much more acute angle to the surface of the sea. In other words the bream fisherman needs to station himself in the stern of the boat so that his bait will stream well down-tide of the others (see Figure 1).

I have described the light outfit he will be using in Chapter 4 and it only remains here to specify the kind of rig or end tackle that is necessary. As a basic principle the trace, i.e. that part of the line which is below the lead, should be as long as he can conveniently manage, and for this reason he may wish to use a 'slipping' device that will hold the lead in place whilst he is fishing but which will release it when he is actually playing a fish to the surface. There are various elaborate devices you can use but it is simplest to tie a flexible stop on to the line such as a piece of elastic which is strong enough to hold the lead in place until the upper end of the lead comes in contact with the rod tip, when it will over-ride the stop and run down to a second

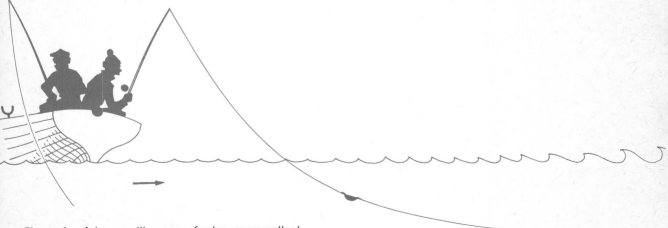

Figure 1   A long trailing trace for bream or pollack.

A catch of good red bream by the author.

stop (a swivel for example) much closer to the bait. Figure 2 should explain this clearly.

The line — and now I am assuming that you will simply construct your trace from the main reel line — can be as light as 6-lb. test, and the hook is tied directly to the end of it. Bream have small mouths and I would recommend a size 4 for most purposes although you can go bigger than this if you find you are encountering a run of good specimens. This hook should be needle sharp. I know I stress the sharpness of hooks all along, but it is doubly necessary in the case of bream which have rather hard mouths and tend to peck vigorously at the bait rather than engulf it. It is very common, in fact, to lose a bream at the boat side, simply by its coming off a lightly-embedded hook just when you think you have it beaten. The lead is a simple boat-shaped weight with a brass loop at either end so that you can manipulate the lower one with pliers to make sure that the elastic stop will hold

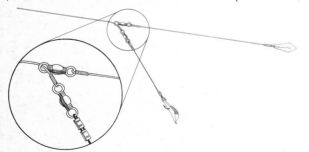

Figure 2   Paternoster rig for ling or conger.

it whilst you are fishing and yet release easily when you want to bring your fish in. Commonly, Jardine leads, the type with a spiral groove around which the line is twisted, are used, but in fact they are very unsatisfactory. They won't release and they have a distressing tendency to come off the line even though you bend them in a banana shape for better security.

The size of the lead is something you will have to judge by the depth of water and the rate of the tide. Ideally you want your line to slip away at about 45° so that you will just touch bottom well astern of the boat. In fact you may find that there is no necessity to touch bottom at all and that the fish are feeding well up in the water, but on your first drop down at least you will have to establish exactly where they are; that means coming up from the bottom.

You may get a knock as the tackle sinks. It is much more likely, however, that the fish will come as you retrieve your bait very slowly, just keeping it moving through the water. If you count the turns of the reel handle from when the lead has first tapped bottom to where you get your first knock, you will have pin-pointed the shoal and on the second drop down you can reel up much more quickly until the critical water level is reached.

This is a simple method of fishing but it is highly effective and the light tackle makes it a pleasure. It is best, if you get a series of taps which result in no fish being hooked, to continue reeling until one has really hung himself on. You can strike if you like, but the lissom rod you will be using probably won't convey much power down below. If you are lucky enough to hit a good bream he will fight in a very characteristic way, pulling hard for a while and then switching tactics and crash-diving to the bottom. On the kind of tackle you are using you will have to yield to him if you are not going to get a break. Quite often you will hit a good pollack fishing by this method, but 6-lb. line is still adequate to master quite a big fish if you are careful with it. You might like to reflect also that the International Game Fish Association have now instituted a 6-lb. line record class, and a good pollack on 6-lb. line could win you a place in the world ratings.

You may have to put up with a good deal of chaff if you go for bream when there are 80-lb. congers about, but I think you might well find your fishing a lot more rewarding than the anglers who are grunting and straining to haul big eels to the surface do theirs.

2. Coalfish and pollack

In my estimation these are the supreme fish of the wrecks. They are handsome, bold, and hard-fighting species, and since they are so closely related to one another and are to be angled for by the same methods, I am going to deal with them in one section.

A glance at Keith Linsell's colour plates should leave you in no doubt of the difference between them. Young specimens of each species are sometimes confused, but in wreck fishing it is extremely unlikely that fish will be encountered in this category and I don't propose to labour the point of identification here.

They are different fish, however, and differ somewhat in their migrations and feeding patterns. Since it is never possible to really understand a fish until you know something of its natural history I am going to say a little on this subject right away, beginning with the coalfish.

Pollachius virens is a beautiful-looking fish — Icelanders call it the sea salmon — and there is certainly something salmon-like about its stream-lined silhouette. It is clearly a fish that is built both for power and for speed as befits a predator that operates at all depths in inshore waters. Big specimens (and it is only big coalfish that you will be catching over wrecks) are a dark greenish-black over the back and the belly is pale silver. One of the most striking physical features of the fish is its prominent, white lateral line, so straight it might have been drawn with a ruler.

Until wreck fishing was established, big coalfish were a rarity. Odd specimens were taken on the drift in deep water, often when the angler had a spare bottom-fishing rod out whilst he was shark fishing. Very rarely were they encountered on offshore reefs amongst pollack. My own first encounter with big coalfish — as opposed to the fish under 10 lb. which are quite frequently caught, especially in the northern half of Britain, on ordinary shore and boat-fishing tackle — was in the mid 1960s in the tide race off Erris Head, County Mayo. These seemed gigantic

Famous Devon wreck skipper, John Trust, checks out the weight of this 15½ lb. pollack.

by ordinary British standards, fish up to 20 lb. which took a pirk lure as it sank in mid water. At that time the British record was a little over 23 lb. and the Irish record a pound heavier. Indeed it was not until 1971 that it was realized that very big members of the species haunted the West Country wrecks, a discovery that must be credited to John McVicar who took his boat out in mid winter — previously the wreck fishing season had ended in October — and found that there were vast concentrations of big coalfish and pollack which came to the wrecks after the turn of the year. Since then the British record has changed hands with bewildering rapidity and now stands at 30 lb. 12 oz. (caught by Mr. A. F. Harris off the Eddystone in 1973).

Before this there had been plentiful rumours, mainly emanating from commercial fishermen, that during the winter there was an inshore migration of very big pollack and coalfish; but it was McVicar's enterprise that proved the point. Since then, winter wrecking has become almost as popular as the summer sport and it is only the weather that is a limiting factor.

Coalfish are an Arctic species, ranging southwards about as far as the northern half of the Bay of Biscay, but with the main concentrations in the northern North Sea and the Atlantic towards Ireland. It is also found off Greenland and the eastern seaboard of North America where, confusingly, it is known as 'pollack'. The fish spawn in late winter and early spring, a fact which seems to be confirmed by the weightiness of specimens in spawn taken over the wrecks after Christmas. The eggs are hatched out in moderately deep water (between fifty and one hundred fathoms) in sea areas to the north and west of the British Isles, as far as our own stocks are concerned, and the young fish eventually find their way to inshore waters wherever there are weed-covered rocks and stones — yearling coalfish 6 or 7 inches long are a common sight in Scottish and Norwegian harbours in the late summer. Although small coalfish feed on crabs and molluscs as well as fry in their early months, they soon become exclusively fish eaters, harrying shoals of sandeels, herring, and other small fish, not only close to the bottom but well up in mid water and even on the surface. The growth rate depends very much on the availability of food but generally speaking fish at the more southerly end of the range, i.e. around the British

Isles, show a faster growth rate than those in more northerly waters. By the time it is three years old a coalfish would weigh maybe 3 lb., and a really big coalfish of 20 lb. plus, such as are encountered in wreck fishing, would be ten or eleven years old. By this time it has become one of the most efficient predators in the sea, feeding mainly on shoal fish such as herring and pilchard. It follows that the coalfish is very much a rover, covering a large area of sea in pursuit of its prey. Only over wrecks in December, January, and February can one confidently expect to meet big coalfish. For instance, the big coalies that I encountered in the Erris Race reappeared the following year at roughly the same time (May) but were absent thereafter. However specimens of the same category were contacted around Achill Island farther south in other seasons but there was no relying on them. Specialized coalfishing is, in fact, only as old as wreck fishing.

If you like, pollack (Pollachius pollachius) are a more southerly, slightly more civilized cousin of the coalfish. In very many ways they resemble coalfish but, although they are bonny fighters, they just fall short of the muscular power and speed that a hooked coalfish exhibits. This is not meant to devalue them. Pollack are splendid sporting fish by any other standard than comparison with coalfish.

Pollack are more of an inshore fish than coalfish, ranging nothing like as far in pursuit of feed-fish. Until wreck fishing commenced, the British angler's acquaintance with pollack chiefly concerned fishing over reefs and isolated rocks fairly close inshore in water up to twenty-five fathoms or so. Pollack occur in vast numbers around the rocky shores of Britain although they are normally of a much smaller average size than they reach over wrecks. It may well be, in fact, that the winter pollack of the wrecks are older fish than the summer pollack of the reefs, and may come into comparatively shallow (i.e. forty fathoms and under) water over wrecks in the winter only, having spent the summer farther out to sea.

Pollack do not quite have the stark handsomeness of the coalfish, being somewhat less streamlined and deeper, but a freshly caught pollack is still a magnificent fish to look at. It is lighter coloured than the coalfish is: wreck pollack are olive-green or brown over the back

The author displays two big coalfish . . .   *. . . and two heavy cod.*

with a dark lateral line, though you will catch
inshore pollack over shallow, weed-covered
reefs that are distinctly red and gold in colouration.

Pollack spawn in somewhat shallower water
than coalfish, as befits a more domestic species,
mainly in March, though very much less is known
about the pollack's spawning habits since it is
of less commercial importance than the coalfish.
Just as in the case of coalfish, though, the
hatched-out pollack larvae drift inshore through
the summer and the yearling fish occupy very
shallow water near the shore until they are in
their third year, when they move off into rather
deeper water between twenty and fifty fathoms.
They don't grow as big as coalfish, though the
British record — wreck caught of course — is 25 lb.
(caught by Mr. R. J. Hosking off the Eddystone
in 1972). The diet of the mature pollack is
somewhat more varied than that of coalfish
since they are more circumscribed in their range:
they will eat nearly every kind of rock-dwelling
fish from blennies to pouting.

Fishing methods, as I have indicated, are
identical for both species, with the proviso that

in summer, when coalfish are absent or very
scarce over wrecks, lighter tackle can be used
for the pollack which are present in great numbers. The reason for this is not only that there are
no mighty, ravening coalfish around to smash
tackle, but also that the summer weight of the
pollack is considerably below that of the winter
fish encountered. In winter, for example, pollack
of 18 lb. and more are common, but in summer
a sixteen-pounder can be counted a better than
average fish and most specimens taken over
wrecks may well be around 9 or 10 lb.

For this summer pollack fishing, then, the
tackle I have described for bream fishing (see
p. 13) is adequate, though the novice angler
might with some reason use rather heavier line,
10- or 12-lb. test, let's say. In addition, single
artificial lures can be used on this light gear —
'Redgill' eels are probably the best, but fluttering
spoons, plugs, and other artificials will take
plenty of fish too. Just as in bream fishing, when
the angler retrieves it is best to wait for the
pollack to hang itself on the hook rather than to
strike it. Typically, even when using a strip of

mackerel as natural bait, a pollack will peck at it before taking it properly. You have to stolidly ignore these pecks and keep winding at the same pace until you are left in no doubt whatsoever that your fish is there.

On being hooked the pollack will dive for the bottom and this can be a shattering experience for the angler who has never encountered the species before. On light tackle you just cannot afford to try to hold this first rush and you have to take a chance of being hung up in the wreck. Normally, however, pollack will take well up from the bottom and you should have sea-room to let it have its head in this initial burst. There is no harm, however, in trying to slow down the pollack's first rush by pressure on the reel spool. Just don't overdo it, that's all. Small and medium pollack may be somewhat disappointing as fighters once this initial burst of power is spent, and often by the time you have brought the fish to mid water the rest is just a question of hauling. There is a very simple reason for this: like other gadoids the pollack is vulnerable to sudden changes in depth which have the effect of rupturing its swim bladder. One reason for using light tackle is that because you have to give the fish more time there is no sudden increase in pressure and the fish is able to adapt and hence fight all the way to the surface. Where winter pollack are concerned this question does not arise so much since even on heavy tackle it is impossible to haul a couple of eighteen-pounders quickly. The main problem therefore comes when you use heavy tackle for summer fishing — as you can, of course. You can use 50-lb. breaking-strain line and three plastic eels on the trace for summer pollack and haul them pretty quickly, but you will have nothing like the sport from it that you will from a single lure fished on light gear. Probably one of the most skilled exponents of this light-tackle fishing for pollack is Mrs. Rita Barrett of Plymouth, who holds the world record in the 6-lb. class for the species.

But it is in winter that fishing for pollack and coalfish really comes into its own, when, even if you use really tough wreck gear, you will still be hard put to it to land all the fish you hook, especially on your first wrecking trip.

Most experienced sea anglers who go wreck fishing in winter for the first time — and it is still a very new sport so there are plenty in this category who have yet to try it — are appalled by the coarseness of the gear which the skipper advises them to use. A 50-lb. test line seems excessive for fish that may average under 20 lb. And that is only the main line. When the skipper goes on to suggest traces of 100 lb. breaking strain the angler is often horrified. How can such gear be necessary? Instead he rigs what he considers adequate sporting tackle — a 30-lb. test main line, for example, and a somewhat heavier trace.

Dropping down with three Redgills he makes contact with a shoal of mixed pollack and coalfish straight away. There is a tremendous plunging weight there for a second or two and an irresistible crash-dive. He yields line to this, thinking he has the situation well in hand, but suddenly he feels the weight lessen down below. He has lost first one, then another of the three fish he has hooked. He lands one and sees that the lures have disappeared from the rest of the trace. What has happened is that three very big fish have been pulling *against* one another on short snoods so that even though he has yielded line to them this has had no effect because they have had a direct pull on a few inches of nylon, and with this treatment a trace of even 50-lb. test does not last long.

He can compromise, of course, by using only one eel, but he will find that this is nothing like as attractive as three. What happens, probably, with the team of three Redgills is that it imitates a shoal of fish which is more attractive to the predators than a single one. If he wants to build up a score of specimen pollack and coalfish, therefore, he quickly adapts and uses the kind of gear that the skipper has told him is best.

Normally this will be a paternoster rig of three eels, although an alternative is a single pirk. Oddly enough, a combination of two plastic eels fished above a pirk is not as effective as either lure used separately, though, of course, when fish are thick and ravenous this does not show up as emphatically as when odd single fish are being taken.

On the whole I prefer a single pirk for big fish and if natural bait is available — which is not always the case in winter time — then I think it helps to bait the hooks of the pirk. This is not quite such a positive advantage as it is in the case of ling or cod but it does have the effect of making the bait bulkier and hence helps to single out bigger fish. When you are using a pirk, it is worth remembering that coalfish — and this seems to apply especially to the 20 lb. plus specimens — will take the lure as it is sinking: 'on the drop' as anglers say. I first discovered this phenomenon in the west of Ireland in the late 1960s and this has now been confirmed by experience on West Country wrecks. It is quite impossible, of course, to use a pirk in the manner you would for fishing, let's say cod over clean ground, when the procedure is to hit bottom and then jig the pirk a couple of feet at a time consistently close to the sea bed. A pirk, armed as it is with a big treble hook, would not last long if you kept working it close to the wreck, for it would inevitably foul. In any case this technique does not suit coalfish and pollack which want a lure to move rather faster than cod do and may be feeding at almost any level of the water.

So once you have gone down with your pirk over a wreck, you retrieve it in a series of short jerks right to the surface before going down again — slowly. You will find a variety of successful pirk designs illustrated on page 40.

3. Cod and haddock

The biggest cod ever caught on rod and line in British waters came from a Devon wreck in 1972, a mighty fish of 53 lb. taken by Mr. G. Martin. The species, however, is not all that plentiful over wrecks in Devon and Cornish waters, the pattern being of an odd big fish taken in the course of fishing for ling, coalfish, or pollack. It is when we look farther east to up-Channel wrecks off Sussex and Kent that cod come much more strongly into the wreck-fishing picture. This is merely a reflection of the normal cod distribution pattern. Occasional big cod have always been a feature of pinnacle rock fishing in the West Country and Ireland but the fish, though of high average size, are not thick on the ground. In the eastern English Channel the position is reversed: cod become a plentiful species, while coalfish, pollack, and ling are much rarer than they are farther west. The glamour of West Country wreck fishing has somewhat overshadowed the sport that is to be obtained over wrecks on other parts of the British coast. It is worth knowing, though, that fishing of a very high quality can be obtained in less fashionable waters.

There is no excuse for mistaking a cod for any other species, even related Gadidae. It is a homely-looking fish with its big head and belly, tapering sharply towards the tail. Its colouration varies between reddish-brown and grey-green with occasional lighter mottlings and spottings.

Medium-sized wreck cod from the eastern English Channel are swung aboard and . . .

. . . are proudly displayed.

It is not the greatest fighter in the sea either. Though it is capable of an honest tug or two it can produce nothing like the tremendous crash-dive of a big coalfish. There is good reason for this: the tail area, as we have seen, is small in comparison with the body and so cannot produce the sort of power that more aristocratic wreck fish can. Nevertheless, as a nineteenth century sea angling writer had it, they are capable of 'a stately assertion of weight' and I have never seen an angler actually disappointed when he caught one: after all it is one of the best eating fish that wreck fishing yields and its current price makes a 20-lb. cod a prize worth having. In the West Country, the cod of the wrecks are fish which have taken up semi-permanent quarters, just as they do over pinnacle rock. They probably find their way there after hatching out in comparatively shallow water on offshore banks. The little fish drift inshore, and by the end of their second year will be 12 or 14 inches long. Codling of this size are shoal fish and grow fast under favourable conditions. Not until they are mature fish of 15 lb. or more, however, do they take up residence in wrecks. Even then they move inshore in the winter, in West Country waters at least. Paradoxically, although anglers regard cod as a winter species as far as sport fishing is concerned, it is in the spring and summer that they are most plentiful in wrecks.

As we have seen, the Channel cod are much more numerous and there will be a much greater spread of size. Many of these fish may spend the warmer months on the wreck before moving inshore in the winter, but there is likely to be a winter wreck population also, which makes it worthwhile visiting these marks in December and January. The probability is that as wreck fishing spreads to other parts of the British coast, and especially to the east coast of England and to Scottish waters, cod will be found to be plentiful on these marks just as they are in the eastern English Channel. However, in the north and west of Scotland coalfish and pollack are likely to come strongly back into the picture again.

There is little point in giving directions for wreck cod fishing in West Country waters There, they are to be regarded as an occasional bonus in the catch and they are likely to be caught by any of the methods I have outlined for the other species with the possible exception of the fine and far-off tactics that apply to bream and small pollack.

In areas where cod are more plentiful, however, there is certainly a case for specialized fishing, and while pirks and eels, the former baited if possible, will account for plenty of fish, there is a commoner and rather less expensive type of multiple lure that will do at least as well and sometimes better. This is a trace of 'feathers' (or 'flies' if you are fishing in Scotland) tied on bigger hooks than normal mackerel feathers. These are very crude creations in comparison with, say, trout flies, but the principle is the same. As they are drawn through the water the fibres of the tied hens' feathers move and vibrate in a lifelike manner, although they may not look especially lively to the human eye.

For cod, the hooks should not be less than 6/0 and the dressing can be a personal choice though combinations of brown and white have proved to be consistently good. Some anglers use as many as six on a trace but this is asking for trouble. Three feathers will give the desired shoal effect and, even though it may be difficult to cope with three 10 lb. plus cod at the same time, you do stand a chance of landing them. These feathers work better if they are baited with a strip of fish or even lugworm (the fish strip is better because it stays on longer).

Fishing a set of feather lures is simplicity itself. There is a lead, of course, at the end and the idea is to hit bottom and then jig the lures through the feeding zone from the wreck or sea bed to about five fathoms from it. Cod don't mass in and close to a wreck as coalfish and pollack do and it is always worthwhile fishing the clean ground within a radius of a couple of hundred yards of the wreck itself.

Of course there is nothing to prevent you from using plain, unadorned bait for cod on wrecks but you won't have such fast action as you will with baited feathers.

As I have said, cod don't fight that powerfully. The only trouble you are likely to have is when a strong tide is running and a cod opens that enormous mouth and kites away from you with the force of the current. This means that fairly heavy tackle is necessary where fish run large — and since in the eastern English Channel the fish spawn in March and later you are always liable to run into a forty-pounder. This means that you should not really go lighter than 30-lb. line,

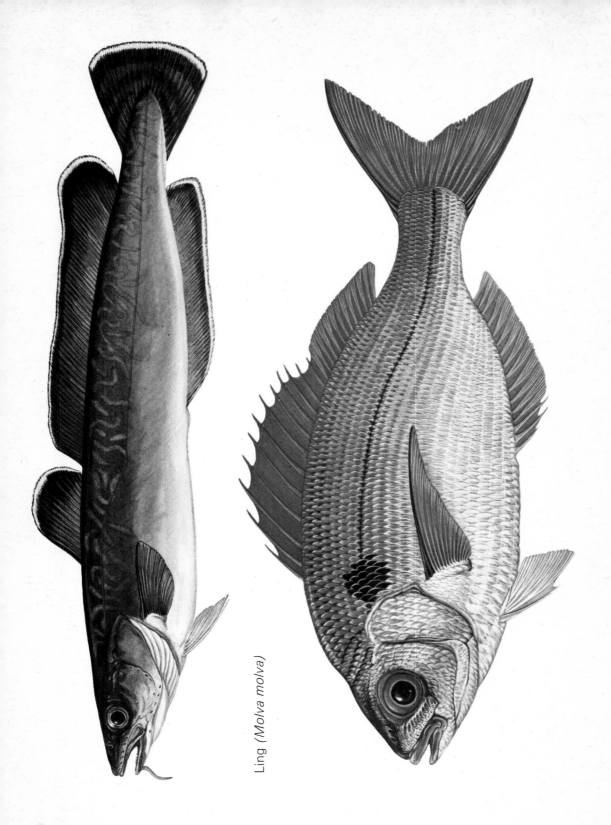

Ling *(Molva molva)*

Red Bream *(Pagellelus bogaraveo)*

A wreck cod for the author.

Typically, haddock is light-coloured, almost silvery, with a darker back varying between brown and olive. But two features make it quite unmistakable: the first is the distinctive black 'thumb-print' above and just behind the pectoral fin, and the other is the prominent lateral line which is curved and black and stands out very clearly. Haddock are a northerly species and until the mid 1960s, apart from the rare large specimens, few were taken south of the Yorkshire coast: their main strength was in the waters of Scotland and Northern Ireland. However, in recent years they have become increasingly numerous in more southerly waters, mainly because of a population explosion which happened in 1962 and 1963. In those years breeding conditions were excellent and there was a very high survival rate. Very large catches of bigger than average fish were reported from such areas as the coast of County Antrim, and by the late 1960s these big fish had worked their way south. Thus the British haddock record is a recent one — a 10 lb. 12 oz. fish caught in 1972 by Mr. A. H. Hill off Looe.

Haddock are not fish you would normally associate with wrecks because they customarily feed over soft, muddy sea beds on crustaceans like small crabs and shrimps and also on sea-worms. They are hardly a predatory species, although sandeels and sprats are sometimes found in their stomachs.

The haddock that are occasionally taken on wrecks (very large fish of 8 lb. and more) obviously differ from the ordinary shoal fish. It is possible that they have reached the size where a more positively predatory feeding pattern becomes necessary, and they have changed their life style completely.

Once again no special tactics are indicated for fishing for haddock over wrecks, because it simply would not be worthwhile to specialize in this species. Haddock, where they have reached a good size, still come readily to pirks and plastic eels, though it helps very much if the former are baited. Usually the kind of pirks used over wrecks are too big, however; in any case the odds against them being ignored by bigger fish for long enough for a haddock to take hold are very great.

At this point I find it interesting to speculate on what would happen if it proved possible to fish with small baits close to the bottom on

and if you are not too experienced then 50-lb. test monofilament will not come amiss in your first season anyway.

Another of the Gadidae, the haddock *(Melanogrammus aeglefinnus)* turns up on wrecks in the West Country, though rather more infrequently than cod do. However, as is nearly always the case, wreck specimens are far larger than the average rod-caught fish and they certainly deserve a little consideration here.

Though they are a smaller species than cod, haddock are rather more attractive looking, make better eating, and, pound for pound, fight better. You should not really have any identification problem. There is a superficial resemblance to cod but the colouration is quite different.

22

This commercially caught cod of 51 lb. is an example of the kind of heavy fish that wreck fishing sometimes produces.

The present British record (wreck caught) came from Mr. R. S. Armstrong in 1969 — a fish of 5 lb. 8 oz. caught off Berry Head.

It is just possible to confuse a pouting with a haddock or whiting, though typically when the fish is first caught (and especially in the case of large specimens) it is heavily marked with dark stripes, although these tend to. fade away after death. The head is also blunter than that of a haddock and the body is decidedly tubby.

These fish are never angled for specially but are incidental captures whilst bottom-fishing with bait. If you catch one or several it means that more desirable fish like ling and conger are not actively feeding. Conversely, once pouting bites stop you can expect some real action.

It is probably the most southerly ranging of the Gadidae and it is caught as far south as the Atlantic coast of Spain and, indeed, in the Mediterranean. Thus, as one might expect, it is more strongly represented off the Cornish peninsula and in the English Channel than anywhere else along the coastline of Britain, a fact for which anglers in the aforementioned areas are not overwhelmingly grateful.

4. Conger

Wreck fishing is already beginning to manufacture its own mythology, and most of it centres around the great eels that live in the bowels of foundered ships. In the summer of 1973 I was fishing over a wreck 25 miles south-west of Plymouth when an angler hooked a conger that was clearly of mighty proportions, and, after twenty minutes of sweating, grunting fight, the skipper, John McVicar of the *June-Lipet*, voiced the thoughts of everyone aboard. 'It's the Big Black 'Un', he said reverently.

Nobody had any doubt of what he meant. The Big Black 'Un was the conger eel of more than 100 lb. that was very much in the minds of anglers in that year. This July day off Plymouth, though, was not to be the historic moment: when the giant eel had been brought within ten fathoms of the surface everything went solid and after a vain ten minutes the angler was compelled to pull for a break. He was desperately unlucky, for the only explanation was that his eel, which he had successfully held out of the wreck itself and worked three-quarters of the way to the surface, had fouled a trawler's nets

wrecks. I think one would be very surprised at the variety of species present and some startling weights might be recorded.

Commonly caught on wrecks, but the subject of much derision by anglers, is another member of the Gadidae — the pouting *(Trisopterus luscus)*. It is not a big fish, it puts up no fight whatsoever, and is remarkable only for its habit of becoming completely inedible within a few hours of its capture — hence the coarse appellation 'stink pot'. I mention it here merely because it turns up all the time, and if the angler is interested in immortalizing himself by capturing a new British record for the species he is more likely to achieve this on a wreck than anywhere else.

which had long since been lost in the wreck and which had floated up on the tide to form a sanctuary for the giant fish. It was, as I say, a desperate piece of ill luck. One expects that a proportion of heavy fish are lost at the beginning of a fight, but to lose the Big Black 'Un when it was virtually beaten was heart-breaking.

The Big Black 'Un was finally hauled to the surface a year later — a 102 lb. 8 oz. fish taken by Mr. R. B. Thomson of Mevagissey.

Conger conger is a curious fish. One would imagine that great eels of 70 lb. and upwards are many years old having grown to that size by rich and easy feeding year in year out around the wreck in which they have made their home. In fact this is very far from the case. The conger eels of our wrecks are extraordinarily fast-growing — an aquarium conger has reached 90 lb. in five years, and wreck fish in the wild could clearly grow even faster than this. Moreover, not one rod-caught conger has ever turned out to be sexually mature. The monster congers of the wrecks are, in fact, young, virgin fish which have not yet undertaken a spawning journey. One other thing seems sure also: congers never return from the deep water in which they spawn, probably dying soon after they have fulfilled their sexual function. So the Big Black 'Un is just an adolescent.

For spawning the eels travel to deep water over the continental shelf — in more than two thousand fathoms somewhat east of the Azores. This means that when they are hatched the larvae can take advantage of the North Atlantic Drift to make their way back towards the northern European waters. Little congers of 7 or 8 inches long can often be found in shallow rock pools around the British Isles. Many of these eels stay very close to the shore, indeed, for the whole of their pre-spawning lives. Very big congers have been found in crannies of stone harbours and around rocky shores. In sea inlets like Milford Haven and Scottish sea lochs they may grow very large, up to 50 lb. and more, as do congers that live in reefs a little way offshore. Wreck congers, though, grow much bigger, probably because of the enormous food supply that they have available. I have said that congers may reach at least 150 lb. over wrecks, though the British record stands at over 100 lb. An

A good conger breaks surface.

With a practised swing, John Trust brings a conger inboard . . .

. . . and his famous colleague, Ernie Passmore, helps him to deal with it.

authenticated 160-lb. conger (it was 9 feet long) was reported in 1904, and since then there have been quite a number of instances of 100 lb. plus congers being caught commercially or being found dead.

Congers are extremely susceptible to cold. A very sudden frosty spell which gives the fish no chance to make for deeper water inevitably results in a heavy conger kill. The most striking example of this I can remember was in the savage winter of 1962—3, when dead congers could be found washed up on beaches all around Britain.

25

The very heavy dead fish have most probably met their fate in this way.

While the shore fisherman would be well pleased with a 20-lb. conger, when it comes to wreck fishing nothing much under 60 lb. is regarded as worthy of mention. The Conger Club sets 40 lb. as a qualifying weight for membership for wreck-caught fish.

The only other fish with which a conger eel could possibly be confused is the common eel and it is highly unlikely that the latter species would be encountered in the course of wreck fishing. However, it might be just worth mentioning that you can easily tell the difference by looking at the jaws of the two eel species. In the conger eel the upper jaw is longer than the lower. More strikingly, perhaps, the eyes of the conger are much larger in proportion to the size of its head. Most conger eels taken from wrecks are dark in colour over the back and sides, varying between a purple-black and deep brown, though the belly is white. Sometimes congers which have been wandering and feeding over sand are lighter in colour — the species seems able to adapt colour-wise very well to its environment.

Conger, as befits a fish with a fast growth rate, are predatory and pretty well omnivorous as far as marine creatures are concerned, and there is hardly a species in the sea that has not at one time or another been found inside one, from whelks to small members of their own species. However, such is the fish population of many wrecks that they scarcely need do more than browse on the armies of small fish that inhabit them.

As far as distribution goes, congers are found in the Mediterranean (where they have to compete with moray eels) and on the north-western Atlantic coast of Europe. In the British Isles they are commonest in the west but found pretty well everywhere, with the thinnest population density being on the east coast of England where suitable rocky habitats are scarce. However, where wrecks occur on the east coast, there too will be congers.

In summer wreck fishing it is fair to say that congers are the number one target for anglers. They have the special glamour of size, and their reputation for ferocity also contributes to their prestige as a sporting species. I am inclined to think, however, that the conger is not as interesting a species from the purely angling point of view as are certain others — very large coalfish and pollack for instance, and even ling. However, this is purely a personal opinion and I don't imagine for one moment that anything I say on the subject will lessen the conger's appeal.

In essence, catching a conger is a power struggle between fish and angler. Once the conger is hooked the fisherman has to hold it hard to prevent it from reaching the security of the wreck. For once a conger manages to get its muscular tail around an obstruction, it is pretty nigh impossible to pull it clear. The tackle used must therefore be substantial, and I describe it in Chapter 4. Lines of not less than 50-lb. test should be used and some anglers go even heavier, up to 100-lb. test.

When a conger takes a bait, its first manoeuvre is to back away, at the same time swivelling itself round hard on the hook. There is nothing fast about this manoeuvre but it is enormously powerful, and the angler can only counter it by putting back into holding the fish very hard. It is vitally important that he gain a fathom or two of line on the eel as quickly as possible and then hold the fish without yielding any line until he feels he is gaining on it and the fish is weakening. Big congers take a long time to tire and hauling one to the surface from forty fathoms can be a long-drawn-out process. Once it is clear of the wreck some leeway can be given in the matter of line, but not too much. The fight, in fact, will become progressively easier as the fish nears the surface and, given solid tackle, it is a very straightforward one.

Mercifully, in wreck fishing, the angler does not have the worry of gaffing and boating his fish because there will always be a skipper (and sometimes he is assisted as well if the eel is a big one) to get the gaffs in and haul the writhing fish inboard. Fortunately, too, the skipper will take the responsibility of killing the eel and recovering the hook, and this is something that is best left to his expert hands. However, if you should find yourself in the position of having to deal with a big, lively conger yourself as it thrashes on deck, remember that it is quite vital that you kill it before you do anything else. The most effective way of doing this is to club it over the vent as a first measure — here the conger has a kind of secondary heart and this should be enough to make it at least quiescent until you can finish the job with a heavy blow over the head. Even then, because it is hard to tell the difference between a dead conger and one that is merely stunned, it is inadvisable to try to remove the hook. Instead the line should be cut at the hook link and the short trace recovered later.

Perhaps I have been a little premature, however, in dealing with the last rites at this stage. First you have to hook your conger and, although it is not at all a finicky fish, there are some points to be made about the tackle, about baiting up, and the way you present the bait.

A basic conger rig is a kind of running paternoster with a short link of wire to the hook, which means that the eel can take the bait freely. In wreck fishing the bait itself will inevitably be mackerel. You can cut a fillet or use a whole fish, but some veteran conger fishermen swear by the head of a mackerel with some of its intestines trailing. Conger are adept at removing a bait from the hook, so whichever method you use see that the latter is firmly attached even if it means going to the trouble of using elastic thread to tie the bait on.

Assuming that the boat has been anchored uptide of the wreck, has settled to its anchor, and your bait is prepared, all that remains to be done is to let down your rig slowly so that there is no chance of it entangling with the main line — something that is more likely to happen at slack water than when the tide is running. The weight of your lead you will have judged to suit tide conditions. It should not be so heavy that when you reach the bottom the line is running vertically up and down, unless you happen to be fishing towards the bow of the boat when this is necessary to avoid your tackle over-running another line fished from amidships or from the stern. All you have to do then is wait, and conger, on little-fished wrecks, are usually very obliging.

Commonly, the first indication is a fairly gentle tug and you should not be too hasty about striking, simply taking up slack and feeling for the weight of the fish before you bend into it. However, if you find yourself fishing without a knock for several minutes whilst other rods are contacting fish, tighten up anyway, for big congers in wrecks will sometimes absorb a bait without you being aware of it at all. Once you realize that the fish is there, though, hit it hard and keep it coming as fast as you can, remembering the importance of getting the fish away from the wreck in the first few seconds of the fight.

Vast catches of conger are sometimes made when fishing a virgin wreck, but oddly enough such expeditions rarely produce very large fish. In fact the first time a wreck is fished the average size of conger is likely to be quite small, between 20 and 40 lb., and it is only on later visits to the wreck that bigger fish begin to fall to the angler. There is a very simple reason for this: small conger are much more active than large ones and they will get to the bait more quickly. The real problem on a virgin wreck is to clear away the small congers first before catching a specimen fish. A second and third visit to a wreck will produce fish up to 50 or 60 lb. possibly, and not until subsequent visits will the very big fish begin to appear.

This has led to a rather difficult situation for the man who wants to break the conger record. Wreck skippers are often judged on the total weight of the catch they bring in, and most anglers expect constant action too. Moreover the cost of a wreck-fishing trip is subsidized by the value of a catch. Thus almost every factor weighs against a skipper spending a day on a fished-out wreck, which is exactly where giant congers are to be found. A day's fishing on such a wreck, though it might produce one or two very big fish, will be uneconomic from the skipper's point of view, and the stage we have reached now is that specialized conger anglers who are interested only in very big fish may expect to pay a premium over and above the normal charge for their sport. Thus, as is so often the case in wreck fishing, the real problem of getting to grips with monsters of a particular species is one of pure selectivity.

5. Ling

In the summer of 1962 an amazing colour picture appeared in the angling papers. It showed a well-known London sea fisherman, Michael Barrington-Martin, surrounded by a catch of ling; and both the catch and the individual fish themselves were enormous by normal angling standards. The picture had been taken on the quay of the little harbour town of Kinsale in County Cork and the catch had been made ten miles off the Old Head of Kinsale.

The last phrase might well ring a bell with students of the First World War: it was here, in 1915, that the *Lusitania* went down in forty fathoms and pushed the United States within

measurable distance of declaring war on Germany. And it was over the wreck of the *Lusitania* that this spectacular catch was made. Ling, as befits a species which is fairly widely distributed over rough, rocky ground from Land's End to the Shetlands, are not an uncommon catch, generally being taken at odd intervals in the course of bottom-fishing, together with cod, conger eels, pollack, and the like. This, though, was a quite unprecedented specialized catch — almost every fish that had come up was a ling and not one of them was less than 20 lb. Barrington-Martin and his friends had discovered something quite new in sea angling — that enormous concentrations of big ling were to be found over wrecks in deep water. In a way they were lucky, for the *Lusitania* had been buoyed by divers on salvage work. The boat they fished from had none of the sophisticated electronic aids aboard that are now associated with wreck fishing. But the point had been made, and since then serious ling fishing has meant wreck fishing. The time has gone when anglers in search of good ling had to pinpoint a small sector of a reef; when the ling record is broken, as it surely will be within the next season or two, the giant fish will be lifted from a wreck.

Before I begin to discuss ways of fishing for ling on wreck marks, it might be as well to describe something of the natural history of the species. Its Latin name — *Molva molva* — is easy to remember, and the fish itself is unmistakably a member of the great family of cod, the Gadidae — you can tell by the spineless fins, the very small scales, and the barbels. In colouration too the ling is very cod-like — brown or greyish above with marbled markings. Anglers, without any degree of zoological accuracy, will often tell you that it is a cross between a conger eel and a cod. This just is not true, of course, for it is a species in its own right, although its elongated body is vaguely eel-like and, as I have said, it is very similar in colouration to the cod. Once you have seen one, in fact, you are not likely to mistake it for any other species.

There is a more southerly species, the Spanish ling *(Molva macrophthalma)* which is related to

John McVicar, perhaps the best-known of Plymouth skippers, gaffs a good ling.

28

our species, but it is very much a deep-water fish and is hardly ever caught in water less than one hundred fathoms deep, in other words much farther out towards the edge of the continental shelf than anglers would normally fish. There is a northerly species, too, the blue ling *(Molva dypterygia)* which is found from the south-west coast of Ireland right up to Icelandic and northern North Sea waters, but once again this is a deep-water species outside the scope of normal angling.

I have caught ling — from now on I am writing specifically of the common species — in no more than nine or ten fathoms on the west coast of Scotland, but they rarely exceed 15 lb. and really we have to think in terms of twenty fathoms and upwards for normal ling fishing (though commercially they have been taken in two hundred fathoms and more).

In terms of its role as an angler's sport fish, the angling season for ling takes place from mid-summer to January, for in the spring the inshore fish make a spawning migration to deeper waters around the hundred fathom mark, mainly to the north and west of the British Isles. Until a few years ago, indeed, ling were thought of as strictly a summer fish but the extension of the wreck-fishing season into the winter has shown that they are present certainly until late in January. If you want to break the ling record you would be well advised to fish as late in the winter as possible: at this time the fish are heavy in spawn and will weigh, length for length, considerably more than the same fish will in summertime. There are certain angling problems, though, in this winter fishing which I will be going into later.

You can judge this increase in weight simply by noting the fact that although the eggs of the ling are small — less than 2 mm in diameter according to Dr. Michael Kennedy — a good-sized female may yield as many as sixty million eggs. The eggs are pelagic, that is to say they float freely in the ocean currents, and in about nine days the tiny ling of little more than 3 mm long hatch out and eventually find their way to the bottom of the sea in deep water. Not until their second summer, when they are around 190 mm long, do they move inshore again. After a slow start they grow fairly rapidly, becoming sexually mature in about three years when they should be about 530 mm long. After that, growth

will depend on the plentifulness of food, which consists almost entirely of small, bottom-living fish and squid. I have never caught a ling on anything except a fish bait or an artificial lure that resembles a fish.

How big do ling grow? There are well-founded commercial records of ling that weighed more than 70 lb., and the eighteenth century ichthyologist Couch relates a story of one that weighed 124 lb. Until wreck fishing commenced in earnest, a 20-lb. ling was an angling prize. These days, though, you would have to come up with something better than 35 lb. if you wanted to get your picture in the fishing papers. Until 1974 the biggest ling from the British Isles was caught in 1965 from the *Lusitania* wreck and weighed 46 lb. 8 oz. In the spring of 1974, however, Mr. B. M. Coppen caught a 50 lb. 8 oz. ling over a wreck near the Eddystone, fishing from the *Anjonika*, skippered by Ray Parsons of Plymouth.

There are two ways of fishing for summer ling, and the first is while the bait is on the drift. The pollack tend to be smaller in summer, so if you use a very big pirk, one, say, of 20 oz. and upward, you stand every chance of sinking it quickly down to ling level. It helps, too, if you bait the large treble hook of the pirk with a substantial strip of mackerel flesh. Pirking is, in fact, quite a useful way in summer drifting of singling out ling. The baited lure is generally too big for the pollack and is moving rather too fast to interest congers.

When you hook a big ling on a pirk your first impression is that you have gone foul in the wreck itself. For three or four seconds there is simply a solid weight that you can't move. Then the 'wreck' comes alive and you feel a rod-jarring series of thumps; then you can start on lifting your fish.

Ling are not running fish but they are extremely strong and, unlike some members of the cod family, they fight tenaciously all the way to the surface. Even with a twenty-pounder and heavy tackle you will be well aware that you have been in a fight by the time your fish shows up under the surface and the gaff is ready to go in. A word of caution here. Anglers are constantly being warned about the sharp teeth of conger eels, and rightly so. But the warning is rarely extended to ling. *Molva molva* is equipped with a mouthful of very unpleasant teeth indeed and careless unhooking can lead to an ugly wound.

More commonly, perhaps, ling are caught during the course of conger fishing when the bait had been anchored uptide of the wreck. Amongst British wreck anglers, as we have seen, conger are something of a cult fish and ling tend to be regarded as a nuisance when they come between the angler and his quest for the legendary 100-lb. eel. My own preference is for a 50-lb. ling rather than a 'ton up' conger any day, but I have to confess that it is sometimes difficult to fish specifically for ling with a bottom bait when there are congers around; and, of course, the same situation applies in reverse if you are fishing for congers. However, it does help a little if you rig a paternoster that will fish a fillet of mackerel at 2 or 3 feet above the bottom. Ling will come up for a bait more readily than congers do and you should be able to increase the percentage of ling in your catch this way.

Since congers are around and since very big ling can make short work of a nylon trace, it is best that the short link to the hook be of wire. The hook itself should be large, not smaller than 9/0 and, as always, well sharpened. There is not any particular subtlety about a ling bite and there is no advantage in striking quickly at a first indication. Just wait until you feel the weight of the fish there solidly and start hauling.

Winter, as I have said, is the time for really big ling and although the methods for catching them don't differ from those I have outlined above, you will stand a far better chance from an anchored boat, simply because the coalfish and pollack, besides being more numerous than they were in summer, are much bigger. They are also more voracious, particularly the latter. It is not just a question of the fish having put on weight before spawning; in wintertime there is a distinctly different run of fish of a different year class that may average 18 lb. and go up to more than 30 lb., while the summer weights might range between 10 lb. and 18 lb. The big winter coalfish, in particular, don't let much pass them by, and they are quite capable of taking a heavy pirk so that drifting is an extremely chancy way of contacting ling. Since the skipper is very much interested in the commercial value of his catch and the fish-hold is filled much more quickly if the anglers fish lures on the drift for pollack and coalfish, it is not always easy to

persuade one to anchor. Moreover winter weather conditions are extremely difficult. You have to have settled conditions to reach a wreck that may be 25 miles away from harbour in a comparatively small craft, and although the winter of 1974–5 has proved to be even more gale-ridden than most, even in a 'good' winter season anglers may be shore-bound for at least one day in three. Thus, although the western wrecks undoubtedly hold record-breaking ling, there are many difficulties in the way of contacting them. A mild January day with a settled sea, a skipper who will anchor, and plenty of luck in getting a whole herring or mackerel down past the armies of pollack and coalfish to sit smack on the wreck itself — get all these factors together and your chance of a 50 lb. ling is excellent.

6. Turbot

All the fish I have written of so far have been species that one would normally encounter over reefs and pinnacle rock in the course of ordinary fishing. It is natural enough that they should adapt very easily to a wreck, artificial habitat though it is, because it fulfils very much the same function as an isolated rock. But the wreck creates a kind of secondary habitat, simply by virtue of its presence. As the tide flows around it the turbulence so effected causes changes in the sea bed nearby, chiefly in the form of banks and depressions which contrast with much of the uniformly flat bottom of much of the sea bed.

What I have called this secondary habitat is not much fished by wreck anglers who have much easier pickings if they fish straight into the vessel itself, and in a way this is rather a pity because there is plenty of evidence that very large fish of species that are not normally found in a rocky environment are attracted by the changed contours of the sea bed close to the wreck which provide them with excellent feeding conditions. They can lie in ambush beyond the banks and wait for small fish to be brought to them by the tide, and the turbulence also has the effect of bringing food to them.

To the angler, the most exciting of these species is undoubtedly the turbot (Scophthalmus maximus). The biggest turbot ever taken on rod and line in British waters was the thirty-one-pounder caught by Paul Hutchings of Plymouth in 1972. That was a wreck fish. Other magnificent turbot of 20 lb. and more have been taken also.

The natural habitat of the turbot is characteristically a complex of shallow banks that might rise from a twenty-fathom depth to possibly as little as five fathoms, banks of shingle or sand which are scoured by the tide and hold plenty of food fish (from the turbot's point of view, that is) like sand-eels. Such marks have become famous amongst anglers, the Shambles Bank at Weymouth, the Whiting Ground at Coverack, Hole Open at Kinsale, and the Skerries Bank at Dartmouth. Unhappily, such marks, often discovered in the first place by anglers, are soon exploited by commercial fishermen, and not one of the places I have mentioned is now more than a shadow of its former self. Turbot fishing in Britain, indeed, until the potential of wrecks was discovered, had become a very chancy business with nothing like the catches being brought in that had been the rule in the late 1950s and early 1960s. Fortunately the turbot that inhabit the secondary wreck environment are not likely to be exploited in this way. Trawlers avoid wrecks at all costs.

Apart from the halibut, which is a rare catch in British waters and is certainly not encountered on wreck-fishing marks that have been discovered so far in the South West, turbot is our biggest flat fish — and also the most prized for the table. Once you have seen one you cannot really mistake it for any other flat fish species except the brill, and Figure 3 should make the main differences clear. However, the absolutely sure test is to run your hand over the upper side of the fish, when, if it is a turbot, you will encounter numerous hard tubercles. These don't grow in the brill. As a rough rule of thumb, remember that while the turbot is almost round in its body shape like a soccer ball, a brill is rugby ball shaped.

The turbot is a fish of moderately shallow inshore waters, rarely being found deeper than fifty fathoms. If you are down in the South West on holiday and you look carefully in sandy-bottomed rock pools from August on, you are quite likely to find tiny turbot, fish spawned that year, lying almost perfectly camouflaged on the bottom, and along sandy beaches seine nets often pick up small turbot up to 2 or 3 lb. quite close inshore. Soon, however, and certainly by their third year the fish move offshore some distance, and, apart from a period of a few weeks around midsummer when the fish are spawning, they come within the angler's orbit between May and October.

As I have indicated, when they are actively feeding, turbot lie up on or behind sandbanks

The net goes down for a good turbot . . .

. . . and its captor, Leslie Moncrieff, admires his prize.

Figure 3 a. *Turbot.* b. *Brill.*

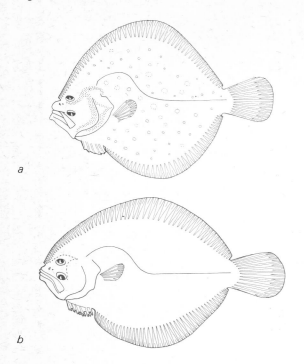

a

b

waiting for small fish to be swept towards them. They don't appear to be very active fish but, in fact, they show a considerable amount of dexterity in snapping up a sandeel with their telescopic jaws — indeed I have had turbot following a retrieved bait right up to the surface. Turbot are entirely fish eaters — even the little fish of a pound or so that are found within casting range of the shore. You can fish a storm beach, for instance, for bass, using lugworm or ragworm baits, for seasons on end without ever encountering a turbot, but if you change to a small strip of mackerel or herring you can often catch delicious pan-sized turbot that you would never have suspected were there.

Unlike many predatory fish, though, turbot are highly unlikely to take an artificial lure — at least I have never heard of one being so caught. However, I would not be surprised to hear of one taking a baited pirk fished sufficiently close to the sea bed. Thus the species has to be fished for as a quite separate enterprise if you want to catch it close to wrecks. The skipper will need to anchor up so that the baits go down clear of the wreck and up-tide of it, for the wreck itself

obviously acts as a kind of sandbank. The tackle to use is a flowing trace of the kind that you would employ in orthodox turbot fishing; the lead on a sliding boom is stopped by a swivel, from the other end of which runs 4 or 5 feet of heavy nylon, 50-lb. test being about right. This heavy-gauge nylon is not necessitated by the fighting prowess of the turbot, but because of its quite sharp teeth. Some anglers, indeed, use a final hook link of 6 inches of wire for this reason, though I don't agree with them that it is really necessary. A 6/0 hook is about right and it should be baited with a whole side fillet of mackerel. The lead should be judged so that when it first hits bottom it does not quite hold, so that the angler has to lift it a little, let out more line, and let it hit again, repeating the process perhaps several times until it settles. This means that he can then 'trot' his lead down-tide from time to time, thus covering more ground. The turbot is a fish which normally waits for its prey to come towards it and hence it is pretty important to make your bait act in this way. Turbot are slow takers, and the characteristic bite is a kind of slow pluck. Nobody ever gave a turbot too much time, so don't be in a hurry to strike. If your rod registers anything after a couple of knocks of the kind I have described, just take up the slack and feel if the fish is there. Turbot will often take a bait and lie doggo, so that you are just not aware he has hooked himself until you make the first move.

The turbot is not a great fighting fish, and you should not have any difficulty at all about hauling even a thirty-pounder. Turbot normally come up as a dead weight except for the occasional thump of the head or maybe the tail, and usually they are far more lively once you have boated them, clattering about on the boards and exerting a muscular strength they did not show in the water. However, if you hook your fish in a strong tide well away from the boat, it can put up quite a heavy resistance by arching its body so that you are having to pull it square on to the tide. Thus, very light tackle is really out of the question and you might just as well use the 50-lb. line that suits other forms of wreck fishing. When you have boated your turbot, incidentally, and you have killed it, it is best to bleed your fish by making a knife-cut across the root of its tail and hanging the fish from a rail. This improves the flavour and also prevents the

Pollack (*Pollachius pollachius*)

Coalfish (*Pollachius virens*)

A blonde ray, an occasional catch near wrecks, comes to the gaff.

white underside becoming suffused with blood which makes it look much less appetizing.

All this presupposes that the skipper of the wreck boat from which you are fishing is willing to go for turbot in the style I've described, and this is by no means likely for reasons that we have noted earlier. Such fishing isn't likely to produce the cash catch that other wrecking techniques will, and I suspect that most of the very big turbot that have been caught around wrecks have been accidental: a wrong positioning of the boat so that the bait fishes farther away from the wreck than normal, for instance.

It's possible, therefore, that if a party of anglers wants specifically to go for wreck turbot they might have to pay a premium charter price, just as in the case of exploiting 'fished-out' wrecks for congers as I mentioned earlier.

If such an expedition were undertaken, then I should expect not only turbot in the specimen class to be contacted but also other species that inhabit the same kind of ground. It is more than likely that these fishes too would be of higher-than-average size. Brill, the flatfish I mentioned at the beginning of this chapter, are somewhat rarer than turbot, but one would expect them

to be picked up from time to time, when the present British record of 16 lb. taken at the Isle of Man by Mr. A. H. Fisher in 1950 could easily be threatened. Since brill are taken by precisely the same methods as turbot there is little the angler can do to differentiate between the species fishing-wise. Roughly speaking, when one goes after these big and highly edible flatfish, brill turn up in a proportion of about one in twenty to turbot.

More common than the brill, however, and very likely to turn up in a catch over clean ground close to a wreck is the blonde ray *(Raia brachyura)*, a fish that can weigh well over 30 lb., somewhat larger than the other ray species in British waters. I'm distinguishing here in the angler's, if not in the scientist's, sense between the skates (i.e. long-snouted members of the Raidae, which are large fish sometimes weighing several hundreds of pounds) and the short-snouted rays. The British record blonde weighed 37 lb. 12 oz. and was taken off Start Point, Devon, by Mr. H. T. Pout in 1973. Blonde rays, perhaps following a universal law, are rather more attractive to look at than other members of the family. They are light yellow or sandy in over-all colouration and thickly covered with small dark spots which extend to the edges of the 'wings'; enough to distinguish them from other ray species. Since these fish are to be fished for in exactly the same way as turbot are, there's no more to be said in this respect.

Very large plaice are another possibility if this kind of wreck fishing was carried out more intensively (especially in the vicinity of some of the shallower wrecks), and another very interesting species, the John Dory, could turn up also. As targets to beat, the records for these species are, respectively, 7 lb. 15 oz. and 10 lb. 12 oz.

Occasionally, when fishing away from the wreck itself, though not necessarily with turbot tackle, one of the strangest species to be found in British seas will be contacted, the angler fish *(Lophius piscatorius)*. This is quite unrelated to the monkfish *(Squatina squatina)* though the habit of commercial fishermen of using the latter name for the former species can be somewhat confusing at times.

This is a fish of extraordinary ugliness, all head and tail, that lies motionless on the bottom in order to ambush small fish which are attracted to its vicinity by a kind of fleshy lure, white and grey, which depends from a rod-like fin just above its mouth. This huge mouth, well armed with teeth, then snaps it up.

A baited pirk is probably the best lure for an angler fish. It so happens that I was aboard *June-Lipet* in the summer of 1972 when the skipper, John McVicar, hooked a seventy-four-pounder which is the present British record. The fight it put up could not be considered lively but John had to use tremendous force to haul it up even on heavy tackle. On deck it looked like a slimy, weed-covered rock, mottled brown and green — part of its act, of course, for the fish is highly adaptable as regards colouration. No one is likely to fish specially for angler fish — indeed, it is more than likely that one's lure would have to drop very close to the mouth of the fish to be taken at all — but it turns up occasionally and sometimes baffles anglers by its strange appearance.

Occasionally, the wreck angler will come upon a rarity, in fact he is much more likely to do this than is the angler on a normal deep-sea trip. In 1973, for example, a dusky perch *(Epinephelus guaza)* was captured, a handsome fellow of 28 lb. This is a member of the grouper family, more commonly caught in warmer seas than ours (Figure 4). Another sea perch which might be encountered is the comber (Figure 5), a small sea perch that has even been known to find its way into the lobster pots of Cornish fishermen. And, even less frequent, is the stone bass or wreck fish *(Polyprion americanus)*, which can reach a weight of 100 lb., though the specimens that stray northwards are a lot smaller than this as a rule (Figure 6).

One of the charms of wreck fishing is that you are never *quite* sure what you are going to haul up next!

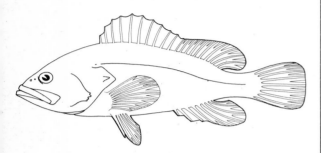

Figure 4   Dusky perch.

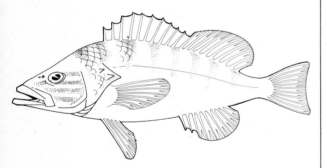

Figure 5   Comber.

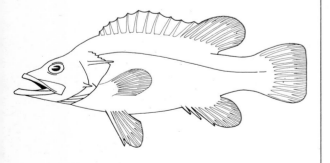

Figure 6   Wreck fish or stone bass.

4. EQUIPMENT

I have entitled this chapter 'Equipment' rather than just 'Tackle' because what you need to take on a wreck-fishing expedition, especially if it is a long one, goes well beyond a rod and reel and a tackle box. I have seen too many anglers go to sea on what seems a pleasant summer's morning ashore only to have their trip entirely ruined by their having to endure it in wet, cold conditions that reduce them to miserable, shivering onlookers whose only thought is to get back to port as quickly as possible.

Even in summer and in daylight the temperature at sea is always somewhat below that of the land temperature and the general advice to take more clothes than you think you could possibly need is sound. Wreck fishing, though, often involves staying out all night and spending forty-eight hours or more at sea, and therefore very careful consideration must be given to what you wear. In winter fishing, obviously, this is even more vital.

For winter fishing and for summer fishing which involves a night spent afloat, you should make sure that you wear a full set of warm underclothes. When really cold conditions are expected I start out from the skin, so to speak, with an undersuit such as the Helly-Hansen 'Warm Suit', a two-piece outfit which covers you from ankles to neck and has a nylon fur lining. You will find these and other forms of 'thermal' underwear advertised in the fishing papers. You can get socks and stockings of the same kind of material, over which you can wear seamen's thick knitted stockings. Over this base you can pull as many sweaters as you think you will need and some roomy trousers to tuck into your woollen stockings. In winter conditions you should top this off with a heavy quilted nylon coat and a pair of waterproof over-trousers. It is very important that you pull these over-trousers on before you leave harbour. Inevitably,

as soon as the boat comes out of shelter there will be spray flying and by the time you have looked around for a pair and pulled them on it is too late. Ordinary rubber boots can be highly hazardous on a slippery deck. Instead, get hold of a pair of short boots of the kind that are sold to yachtsmen, such as the Dunlop Magister type which incorporates a sole made up of small rubber studs which gives you good footing on a heaving deck. Your quilted coat will undoubtedly have a hood to pull up but it is much more comfortable to wear a woollen cap beneath this hood. For comfort I prefer those for skiers knitted in fine wool. If you cannot get hold of one of these, please don't laugh, but the most comfortable kind I have discovered is a Brownie's cap. Just ask for the largest size. For very wet and cold conditions mittens that leave the fingers free are a good idea. At the end of all this you will look like the Michelin man, but at least you will be warm, comfortable, and in the right frame of mind to give your full attention to the fishing. Always, let me repeat, take more clothes than you think you will need. You can always take a sweater off if necessary, but you can't put one on that you have left ashore.

If I have given the impression that going to sea for wreck fishing is a rather tough business, then that is absolutely what I intend, and the factors which make it necessary to pay a great deal of attention to your own comfort mean that your fishing gear itself must be correspondingly tough. In a heaving boat, fishing alongside other anglers all intent on hauling big fish, you will find that unless your tackle is chosen and maintained to top standards you can expect things to go wrong. An inefficient reel clamp or a broken rod ring, for example, can spoil your fishing trip.

So before I begin to specify tackle itself, I want to make some general points about preparation and maintenance. As far as your rod is concerned the weak points to keep an eye on are the rings, the ferrules, the winch fittings, and the whippings.

Paradoxically, the rings on some first quality rods are sometimes a problem because they are first and foremost designed not to groove or wear excessively through the action of the running line upon them. These high quality rings, though, because they are finished in hardened chrome, are particularly liable to break if they receive a sharp blow — if they are dropped on the deck, for instance. Thus although you need their efficiency you must be extremely careful not to prop a rod against the gunwale or the stern, where the action of the sea might allow it to roll off and hit the deck. If you have to put your rod down lay it on deck and out of the way of other anglers' feet.

A flurry on the surface as the skipper puts the gaff into a good pollack.

Before you set out on a wreck-fishing trip make sure that the female ferrule on your rod is not clogged with dirt and corrosion and that there is an easy fitting, though not so easy that it will come apart while you are fishing. Most heavy-duty boat rods such as are used in wreck fishing will have winch fittings involving a screw lock feature. Make sure that these can travel easily on the threads by cleaning them with some spirit and an old toothbrush before you set out and lubricating them lightly. Be sure also that you have not got any frayed whippings. In an extreme case you are liable to lose a ring, but even if the fraying is slight you will be surprised at what a bother a loose end of thread can provide when it tangles with your reel line as it inevitably will.

Reels, obviously, should have been cleaned and lubricated before a wreck trip, and the drag checked. A point that is often overlooked, though, until it is too late, is the efficiency of the reel clamp with its nuts and bolts. If your reel is not securely clamped to the rod in wreck fishing you can be in trouble. At best the reel tends to rock in its setting and at worst it comes off altogether when you are into a big fish. Make sure that the threads of the bolts are clear of corrosion and dirt and that the nuts can be screwed down tightly. Lines, too, have to be checked carefully. The light line I am going to recommend for specialized bream and pollack fishing can be tested manually, but the heavy line, the 50-lb. monofilament that you will be using for conger and for heavy pollack and coalfish angling, needs a more thorough test. The only satisfactory way to do this is to tie the end of the line to some protruding piece of ironwork aboard and then heave on it, if necessary over your shoulder. I cannot stress too often that this is really heavy duty fishing and nothing in the tackle box must be allowed to be suspect.

Thus swivels must be tested also. To save time, because you are inevitably going to get hung up on the bottom once or twice on a wreck-fishing trip, have spare traces of lures made up ready in the case of pollack fishing, and spare bottom traces as well, so that you don't have to waste valuable time making up fresh ones. Ten minutes or a quarter of an hour is a high proportion of the time you actually have over the wreck.

You will be wearing harness — I will be coming to that in some detail later — so check that the

An angler battles with a big specimen; note the shoulder harness he is wearing.

belt fits you before you go afloat, so that you don't have to be wildly looking round for the means of making a fresh hole after fishing has started. You will carry a knife, of course, and I will be specifying the right kind later. For now, though, note that it should be sharpened to a razor edge.

It is no good booking for an expensive wreck-fishing trip and going afloat with chain store tackle. Not only are you spending quite a lot of money but it is probably the best chance you will ever have of hitting a record fish, and in any case the average weight of the fish you catch will be high. What you need, therefore, is a high quality rod by a reputable maker that is in the 50-lb. class. If you have lots of money to spend you can invest in one of the I.G.F.A. standard rods made by such manufacturers as Hardy or Berkeley. Such a rod might cost you £30 or so, but well maintained it will last an angling lifetime.

A good average wreck pollack of 14 lb. from Cornwall.

Whatever rod you buy you should make sure that it has an efficient roller top ring which you should keep lubricated.

That is your heavy hauling rod for conger, ling, and multiple lure fishing for pollack and coalfish. For the last named pair, though, if you are very confident of your abilities you can use a 30-lb. test rod and corresponding line. However, I have seen very experienced anglers who have insisted on using this class of tackle being smashed when three heavy coalfish have hit the lures simultaneously.

If you are intending to do any light sport fishing for pollack and bream, a heavy spinning rod or very light boat rod to handle lines between 10- and 15-lb. test is needed and for ultra-light work a spinning rod intended for 6-lb. line can be brought aboard as well.

Some anglers use reels in the 6/0 class for wreck fishing but I have always found a 4/0

entirely adequate. One of the best reels you can buy for this work is the Policanski Monitor 4, which has a side lever drag, but such proven models as the Penn Senator 4/0 and the Roddy Dominator are very good also. For your light tackle fishing there is no better reel than one of the Abu range, between the 7000c and the 9000, and for the ultra-light fishing the 6500c.

I indicated the kind of lines you need in wreck fishing when I wrote about the various species you are likely to encounter and the fishing methods for them. Briefly then, you want your heavy reel loaded with 50 lb. monofilament and lighter reels with the 6—15 lb. range. There is no need at all to use any other line material besides monofilament. Braided synthetic line is pleasant to handle but offers too much tide resistance and is also liable to fray where it contacts the wreck itself. Metal lines, unpleasant as they are to use in normal fishing, become even more of a nuisance in wrecking and, because the skipper will decide to drift or anchor according to the state of the tide, there is rarely any need to use them. Incidentally, if you have had a tough day on a wreck and have had to pull for a break on a number of occasions, it is very important to check your line before another trip, since excessive stretching can weaken it.

Artificial lures play an enormous part in wreck fishing, and they are the subject perhaps of most wreck fishing talk in pubs where anglers gather after the day's sport. One lure, above all others, stands out as supreme. This is the 'Redgill' plastic sandeel, developed by Alex Ingram of Mevagissey. These eels, by reason of the design of the keel and the pliant tail, look extraordinarily realistic to the angler in the water and they clearly make the same impression on fish because they are taken with greater avidity than any other lure, particularly on days when fish are not feeding as extensively as they sometimes are — when almost any lure will catch them. While anglers are agreed on the efficacy of the design, they will argue for hours over the best colour to use. In the 1973 season, for instance, in Plymouth it was the black and dark brown eels that were most fashionable. At other times the green and silver eels, and sometimes the blue, have had a vogue. An angler whom I met recently swore by completely transparent Redgills — he had been given a batch of rejects which had not been coloured and found them more effective than the

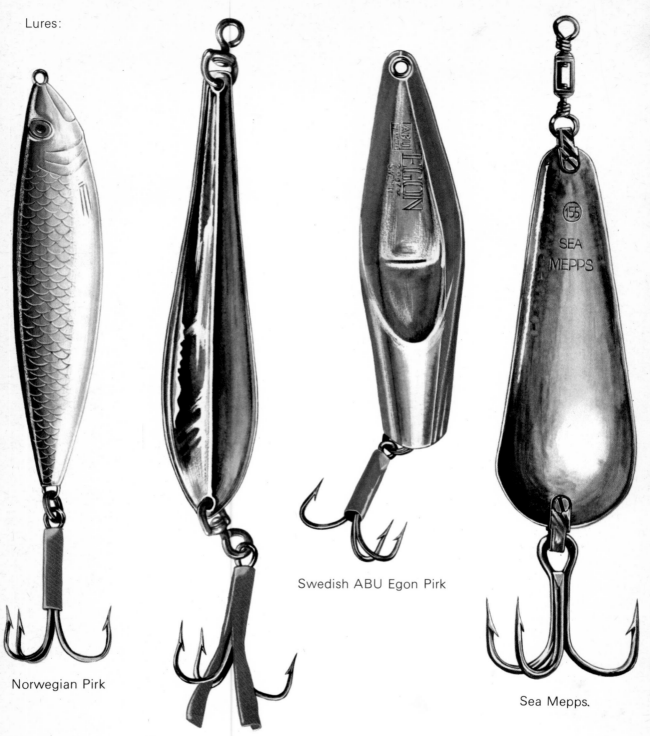

Lures:

Norwegian Pirk

Heavy chrome Norwegian Pirk

Swedish ABU Egon Pirk

Sea Mepps.

Lures:

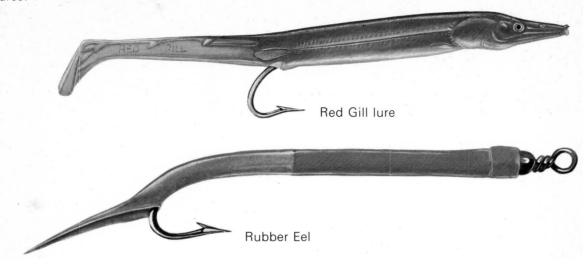

Red Gill lure

Rubber Eel

properly finished article. You can have a lot of fun colouring Redgills for yourself with waterproof ink markers, but to be perfectly honest I don't believe that fish discriminate to any great extent between differently coloured versions. It is the seductive movement of the Redgill in the water that draws the fish, I am sure, and the colour factor is secondary. However, the point makes a good basis for long evening discussions at the bar.

While the body of the Redgill could not be bettered, most experienced anglers don't use the hooks that are supplied with them, but for big pollack and coalfish replace them with bigger hooks in the 6/0 to 9/0 category. This certainly makes sense, since these have much greater holding power where heavy specimens are concerned.

Redgills are rather expensive at 40p. a time when you tend to lose a few on every wreck fishing trip, so that when fish are feeding really freely there is a good case for substituting the cheaper or multicoloured rubber eels. These have been fish killers for at least a hundred years, and though they may be marginally less attractive than Redgills are very worthy of a place in the tackle box. The only rubber eels that you really should avoid are not rubber at all but of stiff plastic. They are a good deal cheaper than other eel imitations but they lack the lifelike movements in the water that soft rubber or soft plastic gives and although they catch some fish they are always outfished when worked alongside the other kinds.

The other artificial lure I have mentioned at different times throughout the book is the pirk — you will find some illustrated opposite. I prefer the traditional Norwegian model, heavy and expensive as it is. Pirks are most useful in seeking out the bigger fish — bigger than average, that is, even for wreck fishing. When natural bait is added to the treble hook they become deadly for big ling and cod. You have to be a great deal more careful about using a pirk in wreck fishing, though, than you do with Redgills. Normally, when you are fishing a trace of three Redgills, the lead actually hangs below them and should be attached by a weaker link of line so that if the lead itself goes fast in the wreck you can pull for a break and still save your eels. This is not possible with a pirk which goes at the end of the line with its anchor-like treble hook. If you do go fast with a pirk your only chance is to react immediately and drop your rod tip to give a slack line, when sometimes the hook will come free. Your reaction has to be instant, though, because once the bait starts to drift away and the line is at an angle you will never free it. There is no sure way of not losing a pirk. All you can do is to listen to the skipper who will be watching the echo-sounder, and haul line the minute he yells a warning that the boat is passing over superstructure and the like.

The range of lures you need in wreck fishing

is not large and this just about covers it. If you are drift-running, though, you can experiment with heavy spoons, one of which Keith Linsell has illustrated on p. 40 and this is a branch of lure fishing which has not really been tried out thoroughly over wrecks. A heavy big game fishing spoon might prove to be a means of isolating big pollack and coalfish from the average-sized fish in the shoal.

For bait fishing on the bottom or in the wreck there are a lot of bits and pieces that you will need. You will want some spools of nylon-covered wire in grades between 50- and 80-lb. test for making up conger and ling traces, although you should carry at least a dozen in reserve already made up. If you do run short you will need a clamping tool and brass ferrules as well. Some spools of heavy-gauge nylon between 50- and 80-lb. test should also be carried for trace making and a box of heavy duty swivels. It does not matter if these are brassy, bright, and eye-catching as long as they are not liable to break. Wreck fish are rarely fussy. It is important to have tested these swivels ashore before you use them and it is a good idea also to put a spot of oil on each one, not only to make sure it works properly but to prevent salt water corrosion. In addition, you need booms for running traces and a plentiful supply of leads from banana-shaped driftlining leads of a couple of ounces to heavy bottom leads of 2 lb. or so. Don't stint yourself in the matter of hooks either. Carry plenty in a variety of sizes, from No. 2s (for bottom fishing) right up to 12/0s. The surest way to become unpopular with your fellow wreck fishermen is not to be self-sufficient where these minor items of tackle are concerned.

You will want a stone for sharpening your hooks (it is a good idea to give them a touch with the stone each time you rebait) and you will want a knife — preferably on a lanyard because knives on boats have a well-known habit of going astray or slipping over the side at the most inconvenient times. I have said earlier on that your knife should be razor-sharp, so that you can cut a mackerel fillet or similar bait quickly and easily. Most of the knives sold to anglers for fishing are of stainless steel and are beautiful looking, but unhappily they won't take a really good edge. It is better by far to get hold of a trawlerman's gutting knife which is made of soft steel. This has to be sharpened frequently and has to be kept clear of corrosion (though stainless steel knives also corrode very quickly in salt water conditions), but a few strokes of the stone is enough to put a very sharp edge on it. For some curious reason you can buy these not in tackle shops but in ship-chandlers, and the best I have found so far is the Swedish 'Mora' knife. Maybe tackle dealers will wake up one day and make such knives easily available.

Hauling big wreck fish from forty fathoms and more can be an exhausting business and sometimes a dangerous one: a heavy coalfish suddenly crash-diving can force the rod butt up hard and give you a serious groin or stomach injury. It is absolutely necessary, therefore, to use a fighting belt which incorporates a leather, felt-backed shield and a metal cup to take the rod butt. When you put the belt on be sure it is as tight as you can manage, because once the rod is in the cup and operating it will stretch. A belt alone, however, does not help your shoulder and back muscles, and a shoulder or kidney harness which incorporates heavy steel clips to lock with the lugs of the reel will save you a tremendous amount of hard work and especially lighten the load on your forearm muscles.

You will certainly need something to put all your bits and pieces in so that they are instantly available and are not inextricably mixed up. One of the big cantilevered tackle boxes imported from the United States probably furnishes the best means of keeping your tackle in order and available, but since they are built to take lures only you have to use a little common sense; they can be easily damaged by loading them up too heavily with leads, etc. Tackle bags are a curse where small items are concerned because it takes a long time to find anything and the contents have a habit of becoming totally mixed up. The compromise I have now adopted is to use a tackle box for light-weight bits and pieces — booms, hooks, wire, spare line, swivels, and so on, as well as light lures, and to carry separately a stout haversack for leads and heavy pirks. Other items — extra sweaters, heavy reels, lunch, and so on — I carry in a waterproof duffel-bag. This may mean that you look like a Christmas tree going aboard but, in fact, you don't have to carry any of it very far. You can then stow your food and spare clothes under cover and have your tackle available, where you want it.

5. CONSERVATION AND CONTROVERSY

It is not surprising that the spectacular development in wreck fishing and the spectacular results it has produced in the way of new record fish should have resulted in a great deal of controversy amongst anglers. Much of this can be discounted for familiar human reasons. Anglers who have never taken part in wrecking are inclined to claim that it is easy fishing, that the skipper does all the work, that the anglers are mere haulers of fish who contribute little else but brute strength. It is not difficult to detect a green glimpse in some of these comments: anglers, like everyone else in sport, tend to suffer sometimes from the entirely human fault of jealousy.

It is certainly true that the staggering catches of fish, sometimes more than a ton in total weight for a day's fishing, and the size of the individual fish themselves, often record breakers, has tended to devalue the merit of hard-won catches from boats operating over what some wreck experts describe contemptuously as the 'desert'. The shore angler, for example, who spends four or five winter nights surf-casting for a catch of two or three cod, the biggest of which might weigh 8 or 9 lb. might feel with some justification that he is more of a fisherman than the novice on his first ever trip who broke a cod record with a fish of over 50 lb. in 1972. I go along with most of this. Basic wreck fishing, especially where vast catches of conger, pollack, and coalfish are concerned, is often a matter of sheer strength and endurance with only minimal angling skill involved, though I should also make it plain that the kind of light-tackle fishing I have described for pollack and coalfish, and the achievements of anglers like Mrs. Rita Barrett, just cannot be considered as belonging to this category.

As far as my own angling year is concerned, I would be reluctant to include in it more than two or three wrecking trips, unless I was involved in a special project such as an attempt on the ling record, for instance, or trying to discover what fish were to be caught on the clean ground surrounding wrecks. I prefer to regard wrecking as an occasional joyful bonus, a sort of therapy which is needful from time to time after the frustrations of everyday angling. Once in a while it is a glorious feeling to know that you are going to be in action with very heavy fish right through the day and that you have a good chance of getting your name onto the British record fish list before it is over. This seems a reasonable angling philosophy to me and I regard the fisherman who virtually turns away from wreck fishing because it is too easy as something of a holier-than-thou character whose attitude I find quite alien. One hopes that there is still something of the boy in every angler who is thrilled, once in a while, to see himself literally surrounded by big fish.

More serious is the allegation that wrecks are being exploited without regard to future fish stocks and that, at the rate wreck fishing is being carried on at present, it is only a matter of a few short years before this new and exciting branch of sea angling will succeed in fishing itself into extinction. There is also a kind of aesthetic objection to wrecking. In a climate of thought which in recent years has tended towards putting sea species back alive whenever possible, there may be something repellent to many contemporary anglers in killing so many fish.

Let's take this latter objection first, at least in so far as it embraces the act of actually killing fish. Two facts can be set against such an objection. The first is that wreck catches do not go to waste, for these days fish like coalfish and conger eels that a few years ago would have been regarded as trash and unsaleable, unless possibly as fish meal, now fetch good prices. Even the simple pollack, ignored for years by

everyone except Cornishmen and Irishmen, will fetch 40p. per pound in the shops; there is a ready sale for every wreck-caught species — not surprisingly since, for example, it is a wise man who knows exactly what goes into his fish fingers. In fact the economic value of a wreck fishing catch has given rise to another controversy over its ownership. But that is something I will be discussing later.

The catch then does not go to waste. Furthermore, because of their physical make-up it would be impossible to return many wreck-caught fish alive to the sea. Principally this applies to pollack and coalfish whose swim bladders inevitably become ruptured on the way to the surface. If you return a pollack alive you will quickly see that you have achieved nothing because it will simply swim close to the surface and is clearly quite unable to gain depth. It must be admitted that this consideration does not apply to all wreck fish. Conger, for instance, could technically be returned, but what prevents this in most cases is the great difficulty of recovering the hook without killing them or injuring them to the point where any question of a return would be superfluous. There would be a case, certainly, for returning lightly-hooked congers, but one would do this in the face of considerable opposition from the skipper who would see it as so much marketable fish simply thrown away. If you go wrecking, therefore, it seems inevitable that the catch is killed, but the fact that the fish are not simply dumped (as is often the case in angling competitions) but sold for human consumption seems to me to go a long way to countering this objection.

A much stronger objection is the possible depletion of fish stocks, and there is no doubt at all that wrecks can be 'fished out' in a very short space of time. In the case of a small wreck, two or three angling trips to it might be enough to cross it off the skipper's list. A wreck, however, only becomes fished out in the case of certain species. Ling, for example, are particularly vulnerable in this respect. They are slower growing fish than most that inhabit wrecks, and undoubtedly form semi-permanent colonies, with the possibility that the fish, having made a

Not quite the 'big black 'un' but a magnificent seventy-six-pounder which won for its captor, Doug McCrae, the first gold medal to be awarded by the British Conger Club.

Another famous wreck skipper, Colin Williams of Mevagissey, stands knee-deep in ling.

spawning journey, return to their original homes. Experience over the past few years has shown that once a wreck is fished out of ling it stays fished out. How long it would take for ling to repopulate a wreck is difficult to say. At present we have no data to go on, though the indications certainly seem to point to a long period being necessary for a regeneration process to take place in respect of a particular wreck.

The same thing seems to be true of conger eels, fast growing as they are. We have seen how wreck skippers tend merely to skim off the smaller and medium-sized congers from a wreck because of the demands of the commercial market and anglers themselves, and that a fished-out conger mark in reality retains a small population of very big eels indeed. Once again, though, we are stumped for lack of hard informa-tion. Do small congers eventually discover a fished-out wreck and begin to repopulate it? This must inevitably happen in the end but we have no idea at all of how long the process takes.

The picture as far as coalfish and pollack are concerned is a somewhat brighter one. These species seem to use wrecks as stopping places in a wide-ranging feeding pattern, and a wreck which is virtually empty of pollack in late summer or autumn can in January prove to harbour thousands of big fish. The difficulty here is that wrecking has so short a history. Will big pollack continue to return to the wrecks each winter? Are we getting just a small percentage of the deep water population harbouring around wrecks? Or have we in the last three years been doing more damage to pollack and coalfish stocks than we are aware of? We just don't know, although in the case of coalfish at least, a highly fecund species with a widely spread population, the odds may be in favour of the.

45

fish. If one is to be optimistic, a hopeful sign is the continued presence in winter of vast quantities of the small fish on which pollack and coalfish feed. The echo-sounder will often show great black masses of pilchard, for instance, and there must be times when the big fish need do no more than virtually browse on these shoals.

Overall, however, the picture must give some cause for concern. Wreck fishing is a highly competitive business. A wreck skipper who has made something of a name for himself can be assured of solid bookings through most of the year, but to maintain this position he has to get his name into the angling papers with regularity. A man like John McVicar will tell you that one operates under considerable physical and mental

strain. This clearly puts a premium on finding more and more wrecks to exploit and already in the area where wrecking virtually had its start, that is to say within a twenty-mile radius of Brixham, there seems little left and the trend is for skippers to work farther and farther west, going down to Mevagissey or Falmouth for a week or two at a time in the summer — thereby, incidentally, incurring the displeasure of Cornish skippers, many of whom are turning away from shark fishing as a source of angling revenue and are equipping themselves with the kind of electronic aids that have made Plymouth and Brixham famous as wreck fishing centres.

Very recently, too, a new and rather disturbing tendency has manifested itself. Some boat owners are beginning to regard anglers as redundant and are fishing the wrecks on a purely commercial basis with heavy gear. This is such a recent development that it is hard to know how

1060 lb. of ling caught over the wreck of the Lusitania.

far it will go but it is already clear that pressure on wrecks is becoming a matter for concern. The Western Approaches are said to be littered with wrecks, many hundreds of them, but there is a limit to the range of angling boats, and already week-long trips are taking place so that distant marks can be fished. The range cannot be increased indefinitely, however, and it seems likely that the limit will be reached well before the end of the decade.

The time seems ripe, therefore, for a sensible look at what wreck fishing is doing. It may not be solely a matter of fishing out wrecks. It could well be the case that the mature fish which provide most of our inshore stocks, especially in the West Country, spend time on wrecks, so that to take the gloomiest point of view, the wreck fisherman may not only be destroying his own particular golden goose but a whole gaggle.

We are not going to arm ourselves with any relevant facts just by going fishing and talking about it in quayside pubs. There is an urgent need for a properly based enquiry by scientists into what is happening. Unfortunately, as always, anglers can look in vain to the Ministry of Agriculture, Fisheries and Food to do anything to help. The Ministry, as far as its scientific investigations go, seems only to be interested in large-scale commercial fishing, which is why we know a great deal about cod and plaice and virtually nothing about conger eels and coalfish.

So, for the moment, until we have a government enlightened enough to realize that the leisure industry and its connection with something like a million sea anglers is economically important and worthy of study, anglers must rely on their own resources. It is only in very recent years that they have begun to organize themselves, and an important function of the comparatively new National Anglers Council might well be to try to discover more facts about the wreck fishing situation by setting up its own scientific survey. The old-established National Federation of Sea Anglers rarely looks further than a day-to-day administration of the sport, being more concerned with trophies and prize lists, so it often seems, than with matters which affect the sport more deeply. This kind of project might deservedly win the support also of the Angling Foundation, an organization set up by the tackle trade to finance projects for the betterment of sport fishing in Britain.

Even if we were fully armed with the facts, however, and knew, let's say, that ling were in danger of being too hard hit by wreck fishing, it is difficult to know what could be done about the situation. Some enlightened anglers might allow it to affect their fishing but it is not very likely that commercial fishermen and unthinking anglers would follow suit. In an ideal situation it could possibly be worked out that a percentage of wrecks in a given area remain unfished, to lie fallow so to speak, for the period which had been shown necessary for regeneration. That is an ideal state of affairs, though, which can only come about when the importance of fish for sport is acknowledged, as it is presently in some seaboard states of the USA where legislation has been introduced to protect certain species purely because of their sporting value.

Other controversies have made themselves felt on the wreck fishing scene over the last two years, and the most significant of these concerns the ownership of the catch. The present situation in the West Country is that the skipper (or the boat if you like) takes the great bulk of the catch. The anglers themselves are permitted to take, normally, a couple of fish apiece.

This, oddly enough, has always been the tradition in the West Country, but it is quite different from the practice established since the beginning of the sport of sea angling (which was a little before the turn of the century) in the south-east of England and along other parts of the English coast. Irish and Scottish practice is in keeping with that of the West Country.

To complicate matters a little further, it has always been the opinion of the National Federation of Sea Anglers that it is contrary to their amateur spirit that any of the catch should be sold by rod fishermen. This tends to be rather more honoured in the breach than in the observance, but there is no doubt that quite a large number of anglers feel that there is something unethical about them selling their own part of the catch.

In normal circumstances there is no shortage of arguments to justify the catch belonging to the boat, with the understanding that the angler himself can take away fish for his own family and perhaps something to give away to his friends. Anglers from the south of England might grumble about this a little, but before wrecking came along tended to accept it. The point about wreck fishing catches, though, is that they are so enormous. Thus, even putting a value to a mixed catch of pollack and coalfish at 50p. a stone, this means that a good wreck catch of, let's say, 2000 lb. is worth a little more than £70. This is serious money and the angler, maybe with a little justification, may well feel that if he is paying between £3.50 and £5 a day for his sport, then that in itself is enough, and that he is merely a source of, not cheap but actually *paying*, labour for the skipper or the owner of the boat. Thus, for some time last year, the correspondence columns of the angling journals were filled with protesting letters from fishermen who felt that, frankly, they were being exploited.

This is not the whole picture, however, and some little thought about the economics of wreck fishing will show that without the value of the catch added to his income it is very unlikely that a wreck skipper could continue to provide charter boat trips even with the anglers paying £5 a head a day.

To begin with, as we have seen, his equipment is very expensive. The capital outlay on electronics like ship-to-shore radio and an efficient sounder doesn't run much short of £2000, and his hire charges on his Decca Navigator won't be much less than £10 a week. The boat, itself a depreciating asset, is very expensive to maintain and to eventually replace. Most wreck boats at present are small converted fishing vessels but one owner is already planning a new purpose-built wreck fishing boat which will cost him £50 000. Some wreck boats go to sea with just the skipper as crew, but a mate is almost a necessity, so that there is a considerable wages bill.

Such figures as these would be impressive enough if the wreck boats put to sea with a full payload 365 days a year. In fact, of course, they do nothing of the kind. The winter of 1974–5 was disastrous in this respect, with boats laid up for several weeks on end as sou'westerly gales made going to sea impossible. In fact the surprising thing is that charges remain so low. Deep sea fishing in British waters must be about the cheapest in the world. In the United States, for example, the normal charge for *half* a day's ordinary ground fishing is around eighty dollars – that is the boat, not per head. Eighty pounds a day is not unusual in big game centres, and for proper wreck fishing expeditions boats need to be just as fast and as comfortable as the ones used for marlin fishing.

It is clear then that the value of the catch is a buffer between the angler and much higher prices. During the course of the day he might have developed some pretty possessive feelings about the fish he has landed personally, but there is no logical reason why they should necessarily belong to him. It is not unknown in some parts of the world for the angler to actually have to pay the skipper to take away fish that he has caught himself.

When you think about it, it is also quite a problem to dispose personally of 200 lb. or so of fish. Since they are your property you can hardly expect the skipper to clean or fillet them. And you have to transport them somehow to a fish market. It is all a little absurd, really. For my own part I am perfectly happy for the skipper to take the great bulk of the catch and to retain just one or two fish for family and friends. There is a final important point to be made also. The fact that the skipper is going to sell the catch means that he has clearly got a powerful vested interest in getting you fish, and presumably this is why you went out in the first place – because you were an angler not a fishmonger. From my own point of view the main drawback to the 'spoils' system is that it virtually debars the angler from trying out new methods and new schemes, because skippers naturally like to fish in the way that is going to provide the biggest total weight. Earlier on I mentioned that this was true of conger fishing – and the difficulty of persuading skippers to revisit a fished-out wreck. The same thing is true of attempts to fish especially for ling in winter and for turbot and allied species in the summer.

Oddly enough skippers are not all as mercenary as they may sound. Some of them, like John McVicar, are keen rod fishermen themselves, and if you talk to them in the right way you can sometimes persuade them to try an off-beat method just to see what it will produce.

Wreck fishing is the newest and most exciting branch of sea angling. For a time anyway it is bound to be surrounded by controversy and it clearly needs a lot of thinking about. Meanwhile, though, it has now established itself firmly on the sea angling scene, and in the last resort it is up to sea anglers themselves to tame and discipline the giant that they have created.